POEMS &

John Rodker

Poems & Adolphe 1920

Edited, with an Introduction,
by Andrew Crozier

CARCANET

First published in Great Britain in 1996 by
Carcanet Press Limited
402-406 Corn Exchange Buildings
Manchester M4 3BY

A CIP catalogue record for this book
is available from the British Library.
ISBN 1 85754 060 3

The publisher acknowledges financial assistance
from the Arts Council of England.

Set in 9 pt Garamond Original by Bryan Williamson, Frome
Printed and bound in England by SRP Ltd, Exeter

Contents

Introduction

1.

Between 1914 and 1932 John Rodker published nine books, and a number of his other works went unpublished.[1] As one of the abettors of what is now called modernism he was the publisher of Eliot, Pound and Joyce, and of Gaudier-Brzeska, Wyndham Lewis and Edward Wadsworth, and it is in the context of the foundational epoch of modernism, in London before and after the First World War, and then in Paris, that his writing should in the first place be situated. Yet until now his books have not been reprinted, his work has remained largely unread, so that such a claim might seem to be inflated. But the details of Rodker's career will not bear this out. Moreover, modernism has by now become a figure of hyperbole, which we are given to recognise in a set of ancient monuments – a handful of monumental works by a handful of ancient modernists. This is a characteristic English view, from which the topic of modernity as a quality of the common life of the twentieth century has been omitted, so that the sense of modernism as — if not a common culture — at least a common cultural horizon has been erased and, with it, any notion of modernism that is not already diminished by our familiarity with its acknowledged monuments.

If we are to look at modernism from a different angle, in plan, say, rather than in perspective, and hence in a different historical setting, not that of the retrospect which sees modernism only in those time-ravaged monuments, we need a method as well as a motive. And that method will be to instal modernism more explicitly in its past, to look for the other modernists: those who published with the great modernists but did not have their work collected in book form, and those whose books have not been reprinted. If we do this we should not look for lesser, more modest monuments, minor versions of what is already familiar, precisely because we will understand that the judgements which originally framed the list of monuments have slipped into history and been forgotten. Just as it has been forgotten that *Adolphe 1920* was once judged to be an advance on the method of *Ulysses*.

When we consider Rodker as a modernist we will find that his modernism is importantly set into other cultural matrices which are less well mapped even than modernism. He was a product of the educational and cultural energies, at once assimilative and counter-assertively independent, of the East End Jewish community which developed after the immigrations of the 1880s. The generation of the 1890s experienced the confrontation of race and family tradition not only with British conservatism but also with modernity (including the modern politics of socialism and anarchism). In his generation

vii

Rodker belongs with David Bomberg, Mark Gertler and Isaac Rosenberg, and with other poets of more conventional disposition: Lazarus Aaronson, Joseph Leftwich, Samuel Winsten, Charles Schiff and A. Abrahams. It might be tempting, using the convenient antithesis of tradition and modernity, to see this background as precisely that, and no more — the forcing ground for a career in the modern movement — and to suppose that the successful were those who were able to make the transition more or less directly. Yet the passage proves not to have been at all direct, indeed we can only suppose such a possibility on the basis of our privileged version of modernism, and if we look into the detail of Rodker's early career we discover traces of yet another and quite different cultural setting, in which poetry was associated with music, dance and theatre: the collaborative work of Rutland Boughton and Margaret Morris, the dance poetry of Hester Sainsbury, and the stylised dance of the Noh theatre brought to London by Michio Ito. Into this were channelled Rodker's early poetic derivations from the French Symbolists, which later, transformed by a sophisticated grasp of psychoanalytic theory, would become the imaginative undercurrent of his fiction.

The case for Rodker — and of course a case must be made when a forgotten writer is brought back into print — raises too many questions, and opens up a cultural history too complex, to be reducible to the assertion that he deserves to be read. Indeed he does! There are poems here which belong in the anthologies, and *Adolphe 1920* is an analytical tour de force of obsession and disgust in which the psychological envelope of the lived world turns romantic subjectivity inside out in a prose of vivid mental sensation. But if we are to read Rodker fully we need to renegotiate the canons of modernist decorum which condition our taste, and recognise that Rodker was able to make of modernism something more than we expect.

2.

Rodker had 'no history to speak of', he reportedly told Pound.[2] To be without a history and take possession of one's own identity is to affirm its modernity, but the ambiguity riding on the phrase 'to speak of' might imply as well an act of silent repudiation. Pound applauded Rodker's guts and invention, but also thought it telling that his father did not have a library.[3] Clearly, Rodker had the qualities to rise above such lack of advantage but, equally, the culture he acquired was made his own. When Pound and Lewis debated the relative merits, as potential contributors to *Blast*, of Eliot and Rodker the comparison was of the men as well as of their work.[4] The comparison, which should be taken in the light of Pound's comment to Harriet Monroe that Eliot had both trained and modernised himself, went against Rodker on grounds of intelligence (Pound) and dentistry and manners (Lewis).[5]

We cannot make a start, however, with the Rodker of 1915, curiously bracketed with Eliot, and between two other modernist old masters, and with his history inscribed in his physical presence — his teeth, his manners, and (we might add) his sexuality. Lewis found Rodker 'repellently hoarse', but added that this 'may be a form of jealousy', and reported that Rodker told him (surely not his very words) that he had written 'a lot of filthy sexual verse'. What emerges of most significance from this exchange of views in which, it needs to be borne in mind, Pound was with some circumspection putting forward the work of a protégé, is that Rodker described his verse as 'Verlainesque'. Like Eliot, he had been training himself in the French poets.

However difficult it is, for want of information, to construct a history of Rodker's career as a writer, translator, and publisher, 1915 is already too late for a beginning. His *Poems* of 1914, 'To be had of the Author 1 Osborn Street Whitechapel', with its cover by David Bomberg, points back to the East End community in which both grew up and accomplished their early work. Like several of his circle in this community, tightly knit by race and kinship but, for its children, perched on the edge of a different culture to which they had access by education, language and leisure, Rodker was not a Londoner born. Bomberg was born in Birmingham, Rosenberg in Bristol, and Rodker, on 18 September 1894, in Manchester. His family moved to London when he was six. He was educated at Board School and then, until the age of fourteen, at the Jews Free School. After leaving school he took evening classes in French and German, and science. His father was a corset-maker, and the family was, to his friend Leftwich's eyes, well-to-do. But Leftwich also thought that the family — in the matter of diet, at least — did not live well, and that Rodker spent too many hours at his studies in what was no better than a coal cellar. He also observed that the family did not keep religious festivals. Like other Jewish families, it was somewhat cosmopolitan: Rodker's step-mother thought that it would improve his prospects if he went to work for a cousin in Paris.

Most of the information available about Rodker's early life comes from a diary kept by his friend Leftwich during 1911.[6] Leftwich found his friend difficult to understand: he dissected plants and animals (he was studying to qualify for entry to Imperial College of Science), and speculated about the relativity of sexual morals. But he shows us Rodker clerking at the London Customs House, and later for the Post Office. Such Civil Service posts were not open to Leftwich (who worked twelve hour days for a furrier, and was laid off when trade was slack) because his father was not naturalised. The diary was intended to record the exclusive friendship, formed at Board School, of Leftwich, Winsten (at this time a student teacher) and Rodker. But this was not to be: their alliance was never stable, and their circle was too large. Already, on 2 January, a new member is brought into the group: in Leadenhall Street Winsten introduces Leftwich to Isaac Rosenberg, who later during their walk together reads them his poems under a lamp-post on the corner of Jamaica Street. But as well as chronicling adolescent friendship and rivalry the diary evokes a complete social and personal milieu, which was almost exclusively Jewish: Leftwich's family knew so few people born British that it was a problem finding the four signatories needed to witness his father's naturalisation papers. Against a background of events which included the siege of Sydney Street, the transport strike and mobilisation of troops in readiness against it, and the Bethnal Green by-election, Leftwich portrays a youthful Jewish culture which (despite his private reservations) was self-consciously secular, revolving around the Young Socialist League, lectures at Toynbee Hall and St George's in the East, and the Whitechapel Public Library, but reaching out as well to the spaces of the West End, its theatres, parks and gardens, and the nearest countryside, with rambles into Epping Forest and rural Kent. Wherever Leftwich and his friends went, when they were not walking around their neighbourhood streets, they ran into other friends or acquaintances, or like-minded contemporaries who took up their *Clarion* rallying cries, 'Boots!', 'Spurs!'. He provides an enthralling image of their London as a permeable environment: packed, pedestrian, and open to investigation.

Leftwich was aware of anti-semitism, of the older generation's fear of repatriation, and mildly scornful of right-thinking Anglo-Jewry. Attached to his family's observance of religious festivals, he was nevertheless ready to use subterfuge to avoid attending synagogue. Yet his Jewish identity is so much taken for granted as to be virtually subliminal: the culture he, Winsten and Rodker were acquiring and circulating among themselves was wholly other – Shakespeare, Gray, Carlyle, Swinburne, Wells, Shaw, Abercrombie, Ibsen, Maeterlinck. They collaborated on a novel about their friendship, to include portraits of the various strange characters they encountered as they went about, and this motive works its way into the diary as well. It records conversations with the soldiers mobilised in Victoria Park, the thoughts of 'Spring Onions', a reformed drunkard who wrote temperance doggerel (inferior to his own verses, Leftwich thought), and bizarre social juxtapositions — a dustman in work clothes cheek by jowl with a toff in morning suit in the Boat Race crowd. With Rosenberg as their example Leftwich and Rodker gave more attention to their poetry, which they sent to the *Windsor Magazine* and the *Pall Mall Magazine*.

Leftwich's poems in his diary are echoes of the cosmic idealism he responded to in Maeterlinck, projected on to a romantic English nature, and we can suppose that Rodker's at this time were not dissimilar on the evidence of the stanza he contributed to one of them.

> Over the distant fields morning comes flooding,
> Purple and yellow and soft-spreading grey,
> Over the heather the gay lark is winging,
> Jauntily lilting, soaring and singing,
> Praising the new-born day.

This pastoral aubade is remote from any East End experience outside the schoolroom, remote too from their experience of open spaces, which in Leftwich's account are more likely to be nocturnes with plenty of people about. It is no less remote from the poems Rodker published in 1914. What route can have brought him from the romantic idealism of 1911 to the modernism of 1914? An answer can be given, plausibly, on the basis of his publications: in *The New Age* in 1912, *Poetry and Drama* in 1913, *The Egoist* and *Poetry* in 1914. From A.R. Orage, to Harold Monro, to Ezra Pound, the sequence of editors has the apparently irresistible logic of movement towards a centre.

But what, other than a modernist's ontogeny, can have taken Rodker in this direction? It was one which set him apart from most of his circle. Leftwich had found Rodker's interests in both science and poetry irreconcilable. He was also dismayed to find that Rodker's literary studies led to a fascination with the 'macabre'. We can see what this might have meant from the poem Rodker published in *The New Age*, 'After Reading "Dorian Gray"'.[7]

> A brooding pallor wreathes about my brain,
> And round me roses red in passionate pain,
> And smirching the wan moon in wax and wane,
> The primal serpent leaves a slimy train,
> An incense dense that, sickening, ascends
> In still-born eddies — the shrilled plain
> Of some torn soul in pitiful travail,
> Then, shuddering, sinks. The darkness lends
> Its horror to the grisly tail.

'Webster', an unpublished poem dateable to 1912-14, employs similar properties ('odorous balms', 'Lilith sways in the lecherous light', 'Shriek upon shriek upon the gathering night'), and extends the range of the macabre's literary derivation. Several later poems in the unpublished manuscript *Syrups* are in a similar vein. There is something belated in the note struck, but it also lacks libidinal investment and dogmatic conviction; Rodker's macabre appears, rather, to encode a notion of the isolated sensibility's relation to its consciousness of sensation, supposedly heightened and extreme. In 'A Note' to his *Collected Poems* Rodker says that he was 'much influenced... by the French Poetry of 1850-1910', and adds that he 'first came to poetry through that language'. Clearly, this cancels out earlier derivations, and we might infer that Symbolism focused and transformed whatever the macabre meant in his case. An association of the morbid and the erotic (but these are loaded words), which might be traced back to the macabre, is to be found in many of Rodker's poems — in 'The Searchlight', 'Frogs', 'Pieta' and 'Lines on an Etruscan Tomb', for example. However, in these poems it is referred to a material context, drawn from life; as it is in 'To the London Sparrow', whose thriving copulation is menaced by the motor car which, by displacing the horse (and its dung), disrupts the urban food-chain. It was as a poet of modern urban life that Rodker first received Pound's sanction, with his acceptance of 'London Night' for *Poetry*.

But from the macabre to the modern was only one line of development.

Another, no less distinct, was in the field touched on by Rodker's contribution to *Poetry and Drama*, and indicates the complexity of influence derived from French poetry. The major cultural passion recorded in Leftwich's diary is the theatre. His comments emphasise acting and staging, with little mention of the play's plot or dramatic action. It is clear that for him the virtue of the theatre lay in an experienced ensemble, a symbolic unity. Rodker's article 'The Theatre in Whitechapel' takes the matter a step further, and negotiates between three types of modern theatre audience.[8] He compares the Jewish audience ('at first sight a typically music-hall one busy with oranges and nuts') for Moscovitch's repertory company at the Pavilion Theatre with the audience of 'some few intellectuals' for English performances of the same plays by Strindberg, Tolstoy, Zola and Andreef, and when he speaks of 'our own drama' it is to the latter audience that he refers. There is no suggestion that he associates himself with his third audience, also Jewish, 'a circle of intellectuals who appreciate truly the developments in the theatre of their foster-mother countries... able to translate them into the Jewish tongue', in which Moscovitch will be 'at home' wherever he tours his company, in Europe, South Africa or the United States. Rodker's comments on race are, indeed, intended to explain why a popular Jewish audience should be more receptive to these developments than English theatregoers. Not only is 'the Jew... the most ardent playgoer in the world', the melancholy of the modern theatre has a special appeal to Jews.

> It is not strange that an audience, for the most part ignorant of every other language save its own, accustomed to continuous persecution, should have the iron so deeply in its soul that the stage is only the mirror of life when an atmosphere of deep melancholy broods over the play. In Tolstoi, Zola, or Andreef they find the expression of all their fatalism, that legacy from their eastern origin and the conditions under which they have so long lived.

It was precisely the *atmosphere* of the theatre that appealed most strongly to Leftwich, and here Rodker finds it to be the theatre's principal means of reaching its audience.

In 1913 'The Pavilion [was] for the moment the perfect theatre', for reasons which included Moscovitch's limited resources: he could not afford the 'elaborate staging and over-refined acting which make so largely for the emasculation of our own drama'. It is instructive to set these requirements of the perfect theatre, that it be atmospheric, intense, symbolic, beside Rodker's own proposals for an experimental theatre, published in *The Egoist* in the following year.[9] Rodker's 'Theatre Muet' is conceived as a staging of emotion, silent because emotion 'invariably translates itself into action', and 'no two senses can be concentrated without one losing somewhat in intensity.' Actions speak louder than words. There is, it would appear, a more direct and traceable development, between 1911 and 1914, from Rodker's fascination with the macabre, through the symbolic, to these theatre experiments, than is to be found in his poetry. It is also surely the case that he would have been affected by the new silent spectacle of the cinema.

Rodker's theatre experiments resulted in two series of texts. 'Theatre Muet' consists of directions for a notional *mise-en-scène* of human marionettes or Dutch dolls, whereas in 'The Dutch Dolls' dialogue implies a more usual type of stage event.[10] Rodker's wish to hire the Margaret Morris theatre in Chelsea to try out his experiments is indicative of his range of contacts in the theatre. His wife, Sonia, had attended Margaret Morris's Bournemouth summer school in 1913, and in August 1914 they both participated in Rutland Boughton's 'Festival of Music, Dance, and Mystic Drama' at Glastonbury. In September Boughton wrote music for Rodker's 'Immanence'.[11]

It is in the context of such involvements that Rodker's association with the 'Choric School', in which poetry was performed as dance, can best be placed. Alfred Kreymborg devoted an issue of *Others* to its work, to which Pound contributed a Foreword.[12] As well as 'The Dutch Dolls' it included poems by the dancers Hester Sainsbury and Kathleen Dillon. Pound makes no reference to performance of Rodker's work, but he saw Sainsbury's and Dillon's performed at the Poets Club. He recalled the connection between poetry and dance 'before men tried to wed words with music'. He also remarked that he 'could not make much of [Rodker's] cadence' before he witnessed this performance of the Choric School, but that he 'then understood the curious breaks and pauses, the elaborate system of dots and dashes, with which this group is wont to adorn its verses.' Rodker provided additional information about the Choric School in an article in *The Drama*, and in tracing the School's origin in the work of Hester Sainsbury he also differentiated his own intentions.[13] His article cites 'the *Encore*, the organ of the professionals employed in the music halls'.

> A party of young women in an old house in Chelsea are striving hard to take the art of dancing a step further ahead — every spoken phrase was accompanied by dancing movement — yet though they at first struck the observer as jerky and odd — after the first minute or two one lost sight of this and the novelty became more enjoyable. One might express the action as marionette-like but with the dolls speaking and behind all a strong artistic reason.

Hester Sainsbury's own account of her artistic motives is cited from the same source.

> I am aiming at a purely conventional method of representation both in acting and dancing, because I think it is the only way of getting the basic emotion or idea expressed without the impure interruption of realism or the equally destructive element of the performer herself. I also consider it is a wrong idea that dance must be assisted by music. A dance can be equally successful with metre used as time and words as melody. Again a dance can be complete without poetry or music, simply as movements expressing an idea — emotional or otherwise.

It was in the latter 'dumb action plays' that Rodker found himself most closely in sympathy with Sainsbury, but there is no evidence that his own versions of such plays were ever staged. Nevertheless, Rodker's speculative proposals for a symbolist theatre, however tentative they may have remained, belong to a wider climate of feeling against the conventions of the realist theatre. Peter Warlock, who sought a renovation in the staging of opera ('realism... must be replaced by suggestion and symbolism'), worked on a musical setting of Rodker's 'Twilight': 'very intense and grisly, a sort of prolonged strain. No one speaks, scarcely anyone moves; the atmosphere is charged with emotion, but nothing happens in the theatrical sense.'[14]

This phase of Rodker's work shows him involved in a cultural setting which is not canonically modernist. What is perhaps most striking about it, in his case, is the contrast it suggests, for whereas Rodker's contacts with Pound and Lewis occur against a background which is exclusively male (Pound advocated 'a complete and uncontaminated absence of women' from the Thursday dinners at which *Blast* was planned), the background to the Choric School is female ('a party of young women').[15] But if we can see the situations of Rodker's work divided initially along gendered lines, the division is not symmetrically maintained thereafter. Just as Bomberg's image of a dancer on the cover of Rodker's *Poems* is not a symbolist icon but the logical abstraction of forms in motion, Rodker's derivations from the theatre, with their symbolist tendency to evoke a single, intense mode of feeling (variously 'primitive', 'basic', 'pure'), complicate into psychological investigation. Expression of feeling and sensation yields to psychological insight and the imagery which articulates complex subjective states. It was along such lines that Rodker's poetry developed and his interest in narrative was to be deployed.

When war was declared in August 1914 Rodker was at Glastonbury, and the moment bore a quality of fantasy: Rutland Boughton announced that a special train from Birmingham would bring him provisions for the duration. Back in London, Rodker moved from Whitechapel to Battersea, and then to Chelsea — the locale of the Choric School. Later, on the run from the military authorities, he spent some time living rough. By political conviction and social background he was anti-militarist; his friend Winsten was also imprisoned as a conscientious objector, and wrote poems about the experience.[16] But the war affected Rodker at first as a civilian and struggling writer; he made enquiries about finding work in America. The introduction of conscription in 1916 affected him more personally. He gives accounts of his experience as a conscientious objector in 'A C.O.'s War', *Memoirs of Other Fronts*, and 'Twenty Years After', an essay contributed to a collection of war resisters' experiences edited by Julian Bell.[17] As an objector to war Rodker presents himself as bent on survival, determined not to kill, beset by feelings of guilt produced by the illusion of surrogacy, and concerned above all to avoid the attentions of the state. In the spring of 1916 he was arrested for non-enlistment and posted to a regiment at Aldershot. He declined to obey orders, there were delays in bringing a charge against him, and he went absent. Within ten days of arrest he was back in London. From July to November he was sheltered by R.C. Trevelyan at his house near Dorking, but returned to London when the police began to question his registration papers. He was rearrested in April 1917, returned to barracks, went on hunger strike, was hospitalised, and eventually court martialled and imprisoned. After six months in Wandsworth Prison he was transferred to a work settlement at Princeton, on Dartmoor. Here, after some months of road-building and drainage schemes, he again absented himself, and returned to London for the remainder of the war.

These episodes in Rodker's life are represented as personal experience of state power — of the police, the army, the prison service, and their ability to dispose of his body as the state saw fit. In *Memoirs of Other Fronts* it is an experience of heightened sensation and somatic derangement. But Rodker also writes of policemen, soldiers and his fellow prisoners as other people, with personal responses to him. And his wartime experience was only in part his exposure to the power of the state; it was also an experience of social abnormality produced by war conditions. As a non-combatant he was marginal himself, a man living an underground existence for part of the time, but London itself was a society unhinged by war.

1916. The War. Practically all the men, certainly "the men" in the trenches, in camp. The young, the adolescents beginning to be called up, the net spreading. Streets full of khaki, but the towns, the daily round, empty as it were. Oh yes, we knew them somewhere, but is that the same as having them round, the living portion of their age, completing the "dailyness" of our lives, integrally part of their age and evening up the balance of sexes, of the generations, the general apportioning of human activity; anyhow satisfying our instinctive need to have that life complete; their absence the starvation of the psyche of all of us like the gland deficiency it was. That period, like a man "gelded" carried on, aware its most essential member lacked it, all its virility segregated, cut off, projected somewhere else where innocuous as far as we were concerned it was launched in immense conflict upon itself. And in that time of intensest compulsions, when that mould which should have cohered us all was herded into barracks, into war; we within it, the for-the-moment immune, boys, stray Russians, Japanese, Colonials, Americans, Central Europeans, rejects and conshies, sat round in a world mad with infection from which every compulsion and "serieux", our rivals, the men of our time, severest discipline of all, had been extirpated.

Memoirs of Other Fronts is informed by a grasp of psychoanalytic theory, and in this passage the psychology of instinct, of projection and displacement, is read into the social body. 'Thus we, curiously, for some of the men who came on leave, were stable: like their women, we were "society" for them, we it was who kept the home fires burning.' But analysis does not diminish the immediacy of Rodker's account. And it is an account, among other things, of his altered situation as a writer.

Rodker was able to write without distraction during the months he spent at Trevelyan's house; indeed, it was probably one of the few periods of creative leisure of his life. When he was arrested for the second time in 1917 his manuscripts were left in the care of Ezra Pound and Mary Butts: they included a collection of poems and a novel, *The Switchback*.[18] As the London editor of *The Little Review* Pound was pushing Rodker as a young writer the magazine should attach to itself in order to establish a claim on his later work. There is, indeed, some affinity between the work of Rodker's he took for *The Little Review* — some 'Theatre Muet' pieces, and satirical sketches — and his own contributions to the magazine. In effect, from 1918 to 1920 Rodker's career shadowed Pound's. He succeeded Pound as the London editor of *The Little Review* in 1919. Probably at Pound's instigation, and with money he helped them to raise, Rodker and Butts set up the Ovid Press, and both printed and published Eliot's *Ara Vos Prec*, Pound's *Hugh Selwyn Mauberley*, and Rodker's second book of poems, *Hymns*. The Ovid Press also published collections of drawings by Gaudier-Brzeska, Wyndham Lewis and Edward Wadsworth. When Pound objected to serialisation of *Ulysses* in full in *The Little Review*, and insisted on the urgency of its publication in book form, Rodker offered to publish it. He was unable to do so for lack of funds, but acted as the Paris publisher of the edition which appeared under the imprint of the Egoist Press.

This set the pattern for Rodker's later life. He was to be involved in publishing until his death in 1955. In 1930, £5,000 in debt, he wrote to Pound, 'It is a nice point whether I should have given ten years to this god-damned metier if you hadn't thought it would be a good thing to have a press.'[19] Among the books he published in the 1920s were his own translation of Lautréamont's *The Lay of Maldoror*, Pound's *Cantos 17-26*, Le Corbusier's *Towards a New Architecture* and *The City of Tomorrow*, and Valéry's *Introduction to the Method of Leonardo da Vinci*. During the 1930s he was the British Empire representative of the Moscow Press and Publisher Literary Service, and was kept busy as a translator from the French, doing much work for John Lehmann, in particular, with whom at one stage he discussed acquiring the Hogarth Press. Later, as the publisher of the Imago Press, he published psychoanalytic texts, including the German language edition of Freud's complete works, and the writings of Marie Bonaparte.

Throughout the early 1920s Rodker was for much of the time an expatriate, and as a published writer he was more conspicuously successful in Paris than in London. But he took being published in Paris rather further than other expatriate writers, for his books were published in French translation. One reason for this was the difficulty of getting his work published in English, even by expatriate magazines. When he submitted his second novel, *Heat*, to *Broom* it was returned (apologetically) on the grounds that it would be suppressed.[20] The editor was no doubt mindful of the difficulties *Ulysses* caused for *The Little Review*. In order to understand the turn Rodker's writing was taking toward fiction, and the reasons for the unacceptability of his novels, we need to ground the direction of his imagination into narrative in what we already understand of his earlier work. In the process we will recognise the cast of imagination which served to differentiate him from Pound, Eliot and Lewis, and align him increasingly with Joyce and, eventually, go beyond him.

The elements of typical modernity in Rodker's *Poems* are those which derive from the life of the modern city: its new locations, new sensations, and the glare of artificial light in which its new type of life is lived at all hours. The poems disclose imagist vignettes of sudden perception, which are not, however, textually self-sufficient, but part of a discourse of affective experience. Working in and through these signs of the modern are other elements derived from Symbolism, which sited Rodker's fascination for the macabre, but which also underwrote an unironic subjectivity. Inseparable from Symbolism were the primitive, the universal, the discovery in the modern of the primordial and archaic: 'the evocation of race memories' as Rodker phrased it. We can see aspects of this in 'The Descent into Hell', and in Rodker's versions of Laforgue's Pierrots. 'The Dutch Dolls' may be written for a marionette theatre, but the dolls are vehicles for an intense emotion rather than manipulated lay figures. Symbolist intensity in Rodker's early work focuses in the self and the person: the psyche is given a somatic inherence, the body made to register psychological affect. The self is identified as the site of experience, consciousness and analysis.

Thus in Rodker we find neither the erasure of the writing subject, nor the ironic objectification of the dramatic subject in its imputed language: both of them modes which constituted the modernity of Pound and Eliot. Furthermore, we find quite the reverse of Lewis's theoretical dissociation of mind and body. Somatic effect is continuous with psychic affect, in a way which removes the new sensations of the mechanical environment from simple astonishment and intellectual fascination. To an extent Pound was right when in 1914 he classified Rodker as a Futurist.[21] Where Rodker differs from Futurism, however, is precisely in not objectifying mechanical sensation. His writing is permeated with the affective modes of the self.

Nevertheless there is a system of bifurcation in Rodker's early writing, which as well as deploying along gendered lines, emerges as a practice of formally different kinds of writing. It is reproduced, as between dialogue and *mise-en-scène*, in the difference between 'The Dutch Dolls' and 'Theatre Muet', to be resolved by and large in the prose sketches included here. Its thematic elaboration and formal investigation, however, were arrived at by way of fiction, for narrative provided the means to represent the kinesis of attraction and repulsion in settings which both receive its force and stage it — in effect, a projection of somatic field and psychic affect into the lived world.

Rodker's fictions, therefore, are not attributable to the mere circumstance of a turn from poetry to prose, which in 'A Note' to his *Collected Poems 1912-1925* he suggests was the explanation of his abandonment of poetry — which was not, in any case, quite so punctual to 1925 as he indicates. Moreover, if his poems were intended to shock, as he maintains, they achieve that effect, for the most part, by offences against literary decorum; his novels, on the other hand, by their habit of taking psychological analysis into the depths of the body, are an affront to the personal and social niceties of conventional minds. His fiction, it needs to be understood, emerges immanently from the imagination of his earlier writing, to develop along increasingly autobiographical lines, under the twin stars of Joyce and psychoanalysis.

But although Rodker's writing is imaginatively all of one piece, its development was far from straightforward. *The Switchback*, his first novel, is not specifically autobiographical. Its plot concerns a young husband's desultory infidelity and his wife's unintentional suicide, and the London of Rodker's experience provides the setting for their emotional vacillation. The wife's first suicide attempt appears to be based on an incident noted in Leftwich's diary, the unsuccessful suicide of a schoolmaster who couldn't keep down the poison he took. The characters' threadbare lives are absorbed by London's crowded and anonymous spaces. Rodker's development as a novelist needs, however, to be seen against his development as a poet during and after the war. This appears to have been quite rapidly foreclosed, played out as an endgame, with the publication of *Hymns*, as his second collection of poems, and the *de facto* suppression of the poems in the manuscript *Syrups*, several of which had been published in magazines. The very title *Syrups* suggests a Symbolist derivation, whereas *Hymns*, profane and sacrilegious, outdistances irony. The two groups of poems overlap chronologically, with a cut-off date for *Syrups* of 1917, and it is probable that the earlier poems in *Hymns* once formed part of a composite manuscript, perhaps the one entrusted to Pound and Butts in 1917, and that the title *Syrups* was bestowed subsequently, to imply the reduced essence or residue of a poetic manner left behind with *Hymns*. Whereas *Syrups* juxtaposes poems about ghouls and vampires (not included here), and popular urban life, with others in which love is treated in terms of loss and pathos, and the beloved is the undifferentiated support of an appropriate sentiment, *Hymns* achieves unity of tone by a fierce resistance of good feeling across a range of contemporary topics. It is impossible not to think that both the unity and the tone, the term for which is surely satire, were achieved precisely to put Rodker's book on a footing with those by Eliot and Pound also published by the Ovid Press. These poems, rather more than Rodker's exercises in the macabre, achieve the effect of shocking the gentle reader. They do so in part by the biological interpretation they brashly proclaim of the origins of sentiment and passion. But Rodker's two most shocking poems about the war — 'In the Courtyard' and 'War Museum—Royal College of Surgeons' — are not to be found in *Hymns*. They are shocking because, in contrast to the conventional *danse macabre* motif of 'Hymn to Death 1914 and On', they provide metaphors of war (as a futile slum hygiene, and a display of surgical specimens) derived respectively from a philosophy and a practice of science.

It is this turn towards a biological understanding of human motive and behaviour which differentiates *Hymns* most fully from *Syrups*. (And it was in the space disclosed by this difference, between biology and Symbolism, that Rodker's psychoanalytic fiction could be written.) In *Hymns* it is one element in a wide ranging iconoclasm, but stops short of destroying the image of the soldier: it was one thing for Rosenberg to write about the lousy condition of the troops, or for Owen to place the dead under the sign of pathos rather than noble sacrifice, for that had the sanction of first-hand realism, but their metonymic displacement as vermin or traumatised body parts seems to have been accepted by Rodker as a step too far in 1920. In his later writing, sustained by his understanding of psychoanalysis, the mind's subjection to the body becomes a more fully explanatory and cohesive topic. Just as in 'Twenty Years After' Rodker cites Edward Glover's psychoanalytic study of aggression, *War, Sadism and Pacifism* (1933), with an understanding which reaches back to his poems about the war, so in *Memoirs of Other Fronts* the psychological nexus drawn around the narrator's constipation and relieved evacuation is prefigured in the empathy with the poisoned rat displayed in 'Hymn to Himself Atlas 20th Century'.

The narrative of 'A C.O.'s War' required its prose realisation in *Memoirs of Other Fronts* to achieve the processes of self-analysis it begins. Moreover, to describe *Hymns* as satire is virtually to define the limit condition of poetry for Rodker's developing imagination. For if satire requires some measure of agreement with its audience about what it represents, that by which it is provoked and which it affronts, the direction of Rodker's concerns pointed beyond such narrow agreement and defiance, while also, but in a new language and with new meanings, opening a way back to his initial Symbolist derivations. In the Preface to his version of *The Lay of Maldoror* Rodker remarked that 'the author meditated with disgust on humanity...a youthful habit', and thus generalises the satiric impulse and retains its sectional function even as he deprives it of social position. Rodker's own development meanwhile was to expunge from meditations on humanity the element of disgust. (Some of his readers, of course, persisted in thinking that it was the natural quality of some things to be disgusting.) In its place could be invoked psychological insight of the sort he found in Joyce. His essay on Joyce's *Exiles* sets out not only the interpretive complexity of a text of extraordinary richness but also the terms available to him for psychological analysis.[22]

Mr. Joyce exploits that part of mind merging on the subconscious. The drama is one of will versus intellect, the protagonist Richard Rowan, a writer. This particular psychological triangle is one of barely comprehended instincts, desires for freedom (equally undefined), emotions that hardly crystallize before fading out. Inter-action of thought and will is carried so close to this borderline that the reader fears continually lest he miss any implications. Analysis digs continually deeper. At a certain moment it is lost. Mind will go no further.

People are built on no plan and since it is impossible at any moment to say that either will or instinct is dominant, the author lets the curtain fall finally on the hero's temporary surrender to both.

It is striking that while noting that Joyce's play touches on the topical question of female emancipation, Rodker insists on the subordinate status of social issues: 'the issues are psychological and no spread of popular education will simplify them.' And when he sets the limits of the analytical mind in its own liminal space it is not clear to which agent the point refers: to the reader, the author, or the hero. But what clearly is primary for Rodker, as the source of the play's rich vein of analytical uncertainty, is the situation of the conflict between instinct and will on the borderline across which they meet.

Rodker was writing at a time when psychoanalytic terminology was still being invented, but it is sufficiently clear that his reading of the play corresponds to psychoanalytic paradigms if we substitute for the conflict of will and instinct the later Freudian opposition of ego and id. What is also clear is that Rodker is much less interested in particular psychic content than he is in the position for identity yielded on the margin between conscious and unconscious, and the circulation around it without conceptual differentiation of physical and mental states.

This is the mode of *Adolphe 1920*. The protagonist's life in the space of a single day is narrated in the third person in a prose which elides distinctions between sensation, affective state and objective consciousness. His identity is realised as if projected on to a screen of liminal events (during the course of the day he watches mechanical peepshows, and a film projected in a fairground booth) which locates time and space in a continuous moment, able to inflect past and present, near and far, things happening and the floating images of oneiric memory.

But if its protagonist's psychological involution owes something to Joyce, sanctioned and elaborated by psychoanalytic theory, *Adolphe 1920* owes little to its textual analogue, Benjamin Constant's *Adolphe*. Its third-person narrative entails no narrated context: Dick and Angela, the modern Adolphe and Elléonore, do not exist by virtue of any overdetermining history or sociology, and even less are they types produced to mount the comic ironies and the pathos of romantic love. They are given as persons with autonomous psychological existence, and are scarcely established on other terms. This, it seems to me, is an unprecedented achievement, for which Rodker was indebted technically to his experience of translating *The Lay of Maldoror*. For the achievement rests in the first place on the phrasally dispersed prose, through which images rapidly pass and return, which Rodker invents to analyse his modern Adolphe. The writing is Joycean in its formal concern for prose texture, and Joycean also in its device of the textual analogue. But whereas Joyce's textual analogy is an epic action, Rodker's is all psychology. *Adolphe 1920* can constitute an advance on Joyce, as Pound for one regarded it, because Rodker's treatment of psychology does not give subjectivity textual privilege: the mode of narration has passed beyond interior monologue, and abolished the separation of interior and exterior domains.[23] The prose which tracks the protagonist's fluctuating consciousness, which by turns traps the contingent to itself, and suffers it as its given mode of feeling, evokes the properties of Lautréamont's imagery, as Clere Parsons noted in a perceptive review.[24] But in addition Rodker makes use of what he discerned to be Ducasse's organisation of Lautréamont's madness. In the Preface to his translation he noted that the Sixth Canto 'appears to be all loose ends; but one by one they are assembled and closely tied in a final knot.'

This assembling and knotting (to be observed, for example, in the concluding image of the mummy's pubic apron, which repeats the images of mummified bodies seen at Bordeaux — imagery associated in each case with Angela), as well as being an achievement of design, is the irrefutable sign of Rodker's modernism, for it serves the double articulation of the subject in writing which does not formally distinguish discursive positions. Dick's self-disgust and sickness have been produced for us by complex and dispassionate art. Furthermore, unlike Joyce (and Freud, it may be added), Rodker has not turned to the Greeks for a typology of human existence; his psychology is satisfied to find from modern experience (in some cases as already registered in his poetry, or others') the images which manifest it.

In his essay *The Future of Futurism* Rodker distinguished two types of modern writing, the formally designed, and the subjectively elaborated. This is a highly schematic dissociation, quite in keeping with the tone of smart paradox characteristic of the 'Today and Tomorrow' pamphlet series to which the essay was a contribution. While *Adolphe 1920* fits neither of these types exclusively, Rodker's schema can be used to approximate what distinguishes it from the last of his books, *Memoirs of Other Fronts*. (But it should be added that first impressions might incline us to reverse their positions.) Although *Adolphe 1920* might be fitted out with biographical reference, and read as a *roman-à-clef* and an act of self-analysis, the effort would hardly be worth our while, and indeed would inhibit our appreciation of its objectification as a work of art. Its protagonist is denoted by the text as completely as are his psychic states by his body and its extension into the lived world. *Memoirs of Other Fronts*, on the other hand, asks to be read as autobiography treated as fiction. Rodker writes anonymously in the first person, and the narrative turns largely on his wartime experience, in part incorporated from 'A C.O.'s War' (which provides the title for the middle section) and *Dartmoor*. This in fact comprises the major portion of the *Memoirs*, and is flanked by shorter sections which deal with the narrator's relations with two women, Olivia and Muriel. The book is not, however, a sport growing wildly from the genre of war memoir. The war is represented as one aspect of a more general crisis of civilisation, manifested on more than one front and not confined by the dates 1914 and 1918. This crisis is construed in terms of individual psychology, but with the sense, not touched upon in *Adolphe 1920*, that it is to be read back into the pathology of social life. By means of a carefully plotted temporal sequence, and its darting penetration by the recollection of people and places, the period of the *Memoirs* (1914-28) is given an epochal unity which does not depend on chronology. Others appear to the narrator as loose ends of experience and then as complex knots of relationship, and thus the disjunctive narrative sequence is psychologically underpinned. Psychological analysis is explicitly narratorial, as it was not in

Adolphe 1920. The *Memoirs* close on the image of the narrator's daughter, 'a child cast out, deserted by first one parent, then by the other' — as, significantly, had been Olivia. This complicates the figural knotting of *Adolphe 1920* to return psychology to society and history, and to the future, in what begs to be read as a new form of hope invested in the human understanding achieved by psychoanalysis. This hope, embodied in the very structure of the narrative, is also figured extensively in its retrospect of a life that has changed — for the better — with time and age.

It is this note of hope tempered by experience that was caught by Bomberg in his comment on his portrait of Rodker at this time. 'I paint him at thirty-six in the mood of our friendship in youth — a sympathetic forbearing from Malice and with a tolerance of his burden on earth.'[25]

3.

Discretion required that *Memoirs of Other Fronts* be published anonymously, hardly an opportune conclusion to the public career of a writer whose work was already little known. But Rodker's history as a writer was also brought to a close in synchrony with political and economic events which spelled the end of modernism. He did not continue as one of its elder statesmen, and died too soon to be sought out by its historians. But his writing is a genuine and distinguished achievement, which can add to our understanding of modernism both by uncovering the complexity of its origins and by showing how, under his hand, it was able to incorporate the insights of psychoanalysis without converting its imagery into literary symbols. As in the best of Pound's poetry, symbolism is translated back into the world of the senses, but in Rodker's writing it takes on also a hallucinatory mental vividness.

This edition is intended to make a selection of John Rodker's writing available to late twentieth century readers, and the choice of texts was restricted, for the reason which guided the editorial treatment of his poems, mentioned below, to published works in English. Some previously unpublished poems have, however, been included.

There are three groups of material on which to base an edition of Rodker's poems: his three published volumes; publications in anthologies and magazines; and his verse manuscripts in the Marianne Rodker Collection at the Harry Ransom Humanities Research Center, University of Texas at Austin. The manuscript material is extensive and includes two unpublished collections of poetry. The first of these, *Syrups*, consists of poems written between 1914 and 1917, and was put together in part from corrected and revised magazine pages; as I suggest above, it is likely that Rodker removed material from this manuscript when the copy for *Hymns* was put together. The second unpublished collection, *Pieta and Other Poems*, is an enlargement of *Collected Poems 1912-1925*, dateable to the early 1930s, and includes translations from Pierre-Jean Jouve's *Sueurs de Sang*. *Collected Poems 1912-1925* was the excessively rigorous selection — only twenty-eight poems — of a writer who had outgrown poetry, and abandoned it for prose. It represents the author's final intention towards only a few of the poems he wrote, and does not (as the existence of the second unpublished collection demonstrates) represent his final intention towards his corpus of poetry. As one purpose of an edition such as this is to restore an overlooked writer to history, a guiding editorial principle has been to restore Rodker's text, as far as possible, to its historical context of publication. This edition of his poems is based in the first place, therefore, on *Poems* and *Hymns*, which are reprinted integrally. 'Theatre Muet', 'The Dutch Dolls', a group of prose sketches and poems, and other poems, are included in separate sections. These have been collected from magazine, anthology and manuscript sources, with preference given to the latter as a source of copy text for the reasons outlined below.

Rodker's poems, as Pound noted in his remarks on the Choric School, make extensive use of two unorthodox punctuation marks, the dash and the ellipsis. In his manuscripts the signs for these are not consistent: dashes are sometimes marked only by a hyphen, ellipses sometimes by two, sometimes by four points. The spacing of these signs is no less inconsistent. Printers dealt with these according to house styles or personal whim or sometimes ignored them altogether. For this edition the dash has been normalised as a spaced em rule, and the ellipsis as three points.

Adolphe 1920 follows the text of the Aquila Press edition, in which the omission of inverted commas from contractions is carried through consistently as it was not in the serial publication in *The Exile*. This orthographical convention has been retained as intrinsic to the text. It occurs mostly in passages of direct speech (which is not marked by inverted commas), rarely causes the reader to hesitate, and has a definite function to perform.

ANDREW CROZIER

Acknowledgements

It is not too far-fetched, I think, to record an initial debt, even if at second hand, to Ezra Pound, whose *Letters* provided the stimulus to seek out and collect John Rodker's writings; it is pleasant, in any case, to be able to acknowledge a particular debt in addition to the general indebtedness I, like so many others, feel to his work.

My greatest debt, however, is to Joan Rodker, for permission to prepare this edition of her father's writings, and for patience in the face of persistent enquiries and slow progress. This edition would not exist without her interest and support, and I hope that my work is an adequate measure of the gratitude I feel.

I am grateful to Camilla Bagg for recollections of her father, and to David Burton, the late Jack Lindsay, the late Kathleen Dillon Morrison, Mrs K. Phillips, Herta Ryder, and the late Charles Schiff for their recollections of John Rodker at different periods of his life. I am also grateful, for specific information, to Nathalie Blondel (about Mary Butts), the late H.M. Crozier (about Florence Upton), Michael Hurd (about Rodker and Rutland Boughton), and Peter Tucker (about Hester Sainsbury). John Martin's gift of a copy of the sheet music of Boughton's setting of 'Immanence' pointed my research in a new direction.

Various friends, colleagues, and strangers have helped with advice or discussion, and in other more practical ways, and I thank Barry Ahearn, Elaine Bate, the late George Butterick, Robert Byington, Bruce Clarke, Roger L. Conover, Richard Cork, Bill Fishman, Mark Glazebrook, Jessica Gould, Julia Keddle, the late John Lehmann, Jane Lidderdale, Jean Liddiard, Tony Lopez, D.S. Marriott, Ian Patterson, Paul Rassam, Stephen Rodefer, Edouard Roditi, Anthony Rota, Anthony Rudolf, John Seed, Charles Swann, Patrick Wright and Charles Watts.

I am grateful to the late Sala Leftwich for permission to quote from her husband's diary; to the Harry Ransom Humanities Research Center, University of Texas, Austin, for permission to publish material from the Marianne Rodker collection; and to the Beinecke Rare Book and Manuscript Library, Yale University, for permission to quote from a letter of Rodker's in the Ezra Pound papers. I am grateful also for assistance from the Department of Rare Books, Cornell University Library; the Joseph Regenstein Library, University of Chicago; the Houghton Library, Harvard University; the Department of Documents, Imperial War Museum; the Lilly Library, Indiana University; the Poetry/Rare Books Collection, State University of New York at Buffalo; the Berg Collection, New York Public Library; Princeton University Library; the University of Sussex Library; the Alderman Library, University of Virginia; the Frumkin Memorial Collection, Golda Meir Library, University of Wisconsin-Milwaukee; and to the School of English and American Studies, University of Sussex, for support from its research funds.

Poems

POEMS (1914)

The Poet to his Poems

Introduction to his First Volume

'Poets starve so near the stars
Because they like to think of bars
Of pure bright gold near them in heaven,...
And things we hardly understand,
Like mystic numbers three and seven —
And all the things we know are dead
In a dead land.
They talk of brains from which "thought bled" —
Poor stricken brains — what could they mean?
We're very happy here; we've been
Through love and life and such like things,
And have not burst our hearts —
If our loves leave us, what of that?
There's no wound smarts
Forever.... If our life's flat
It's only that we cannot spend
All we would....
Now should this poet lend
Us something... (if he could),...
We'd show him life more splendid far
Than all his dreams or poems are.'

A Slice of Life

The sky broods over the river —
The waves tumble and flee.
And down go the dead things ever
Down to the sea.

A dog, an empty keg,
An outworn hat.
And with a broken leg
A pregnant cat.

In the Strand

Desperate and disdainful showed his wares, ...
Stupid things, ... laces, studs, ...
I bought ... his look ... and this verse.

The Gas Flame

To Kathleen Dillon

This yellow, flickering flame
That endless anguished writhes — in endless obscure pain
Contorted.... Thrusting ever upwards till the brain
Swoons with its arid pallor, feeling it flicker, ... aim
High ... and ashrill for clean air.... It came
Bursting upon its stalk, and sudden drooping in sick bloom
Poured down the room;
Trickling into the obscure, obscene places where the brain reels;
Incredibly mute, its pallor weaves me fire,
Bursting and searing the lead eye-balls with false wheels
That grate forever, clashing meet and sudden....
Nothing.... Then again it writhes and stands incredibly mute,
Swaying in a little weary spire
So very faint....
There is a tale of Arcady, ... but no ...
This bloom, this shuddering bloom
That trickles into the obscure, obscene places
Making the brain reel....
There is a tale of Arcady ... with marshes ...
And swallows three that headlong wheel ...
And ... faces....
But no.... This bloom, this shuddering, drooping bloom
That trickles into the brain's obscure, obscene places,
With clatter of the first boot on the floor
And darkness surging sore on brains like ours....
Will no one pluck the bloom, the magic, weary bloom
That blows but once, ere night droops
Very weary in after the long war....
There is a tale of Arcady....

Soria Moria

Beyond the soul's edges...

Drily whisper the sedges.
Patches of the lake gleam mournful white....
There is a hint of billowing towers
And the swish of huddling trees....
But the lake glimmers in the moonlight,
And in some sad places is so giddily deep....

Laughter and jangle of bells,...
And something asleep....

Laughter and jangle of bells
Beyond the soul's edges....

Immanence

Cool water pours
Into dim silence.
Through the tense shade
The musk of far roses
Gloses
The sense....

Cool water pours...
Dissolving thin sleep
From the corners of mind....
But the eyes are more blind
And the slumber more deep....

The fierce heart o' the rose
Bursts in the sun....

...cool...water...pours.

The Music Hall

The group soul anguished drives up to the vane;
Shivers over the clamant band,
And tremulously sinks upon its padded seat, . . .
With such a pleasant shiver of the bowels.
(The first faint peristalt . . .)
And a thin hunger somewhere.
Beauty or woman; something not over-rare
That will absorb the thrill, the gushing energic thrill. . . .
We watch and smoke . . . our trembling hands
That flutter for a space an arc of light
With acrid trailing fume. . . .
But oh . . . the hunger. . . .

*. . . for the soul is as a little bird mounting to heaven rejoicing, when the bars
of thought, which are its cage, lie broken about it. . . .*

There is a little room inside my mind
With mirrors lined . . .
It must be like the eye of some huge fly. . . .

Whoever enters there swoons deep and deep . . .
So deep, the scared soul quite forgets to weep . . .
And wonders at itself. . . . By and bye

Breasting the night . . . it will forget
How distant thrust the light . . . how wet
And comforting it drenched him; who might not descry

Nor place nor footing in that blackness . . . ah! so frail . . .
Where scaur and precipice were mirrored pale
Drifting in icy darkness pitifully . . .

And marvel at the horror of the sight
He barely may recall . . . one light
Bursting upon one mirror —

Then mirror unto mirror . . . till he saw
That swart and anguished wriggling thing;
His soul . . . take wing . . .

And ever mounting; higher and more high
Warble a song of joy . . . so glad
That being found it too might fructify.

8

Under the Trees, II

It is so desolate:
This blown leaf softly falling,
Without sound — and helpless.
Each little wind thrills it —
Still without sound.
Not a bird sings...
Not a leaf stirs...
Suddenly the tawny brothers whisper
And are silent.
A long thin silence....
The twilight grows,
And now and then the little brothers whisper,
And stir softly,
And lie still....
 'Come little sister,
You will sleep in a bed all agolden.'
 One star hides in a tree top
From its pale mother,
The little far moon,
Who washes the spangles
From her caught children....
Poor stars....
Little sad wind
O touch my hair.

Under the Trees, III

Wind waking in the leaves —
It is cold...
And pass wings?

Wind waking in the leaves.
Each cold star burns them
Till they stir
Under its spear.

Wind waking
Sad
And pitiful.

Consummation

She was so tired after the night.
Out of a dream all things grew utter white,
And calm with peace beyond imagining.
With one bird brooding there that dared not sing
But preened one wing.

Out of the widening white haze
Desire now mocked her. All her virgin days
Swung thin and shrivelled; in lush undergrowth
Made ponderous her limbs — and at her mouth
Bittered her lips with drouth.

Yet sweet the bitterness thereof
When each limb had sucked full from limbs of love.
Breast from soft breast and thigh from urgent thigh
And lip from lip... while night passed by
Most wearily.

Leaving the needless heart to labour on:
Though life grew vain when the dear lust was gone,
And yet too tired to wish for Death at all.

The Mercury Vapour Lamps

At evening the blossom of the sun is blown;
Its wantoned vivid music is not heard.
Its perfume from the earth for one short night is flown.

Then does its spawn at some dark word
Swarm into many coloured bloom... clustring more strange
Than any shape that any man may know
In all those spacious heavenly fields, where change
Unending the world-stars... where all is flow
And ceaseless passionate call and counter-call.

    Here where each spore bursts, where fall
From some, swift-shooting stars, strong shreds of light.
Where some among them whisper in the night;
Some whistle shrill... some hiss and click,

And mutter fearfully, some trick
Themselves in scarlet; some in gold.
And there are those which stamens hold
Fiery serpents fold on fold.

Now does the bloom that guards the night creep out.
It writhes from out its nest. Its pallid flow
Etiolates the dark: its sullen glow
Pierces thro' all things. Now the shout
And bustle grow more sinister; the street
Glooms pale and waste as any place in hell.
While at the hurrying feet
Clatters the chase of those proud souls that fell.

It striketh to the heart. It shards the flesh.
The livid faces speak the livid soul;
And each soul shows it livid in the mesh.
Yet will your love not pass through whole.
Her smile shall come two violet back-writhed lips
Round pallid teeth; and her dead hips
Shall no more flex for you . . . ah! the killed joy.
Yet glad in this, Love cannot more make happy or annoy.

    O! it is subtle this:
This monstrous spawning of the sun with man.
That cankers in sweet flesh and in each kiss;
And leaves us wandering, all wan
And purposeless within this bruit . . . where none dare wait.

Yet hurrying is quite lost . . . the spate
Takes speed . . . and noise . . .

Like a huge worm it sprawls,
Some orchis tangled in some monstrous place.
Where the far light comes trembling under the vast walls
That stretch forever . . .
                              Yet . . . for a space
Music will rise; a pæan from the sun
Though Death creep down 'ere twilight is begun.

Sleep-Sick

Joy has gone out from me — and warmth —
And whether she sleep or no
It matters not...
Or whether the sleep be long
I will not heed...
For my lids grow heavy as night is
Without stars.

Have I not offered up my hours before her pain
Till all my days went thin as her own pain?
And now my lids grow heavy as night is
Without stars...
And she sleeps.

Whether she sleep or no
I must not heed
Lest I wake.

Whether she sleep or no
I will not heed...
Or whether the sleep be long
I care not now.

Spelled

Peering through the tangle of her hair
I saw
The sun shafts
Splintering.

The enchanted web
That was all bronze.

And in cool deeps behind
I dreamed...
While the warm shafts
Splintered
On that enchanted web
Which was all golden
Against my eyes.

Till blood grew thin.

The Storm

No wind in all that place.
Only the sun beating down.
Like sleepy cats we moved within the shade.

And when I touched him
Such a thrill went through my arm
And ceased where my ring was....
It left me tingling....
The air was so full charged
Of the electric force,
It overflowed in mystic flare.
Pale blue, it dazed the sky
Pale blue
And vast
It challenged all the sky.

In the evening
A small chill wind
Brought back the moisture to our veins of wilted flowers.

The rain came
Swarming.

Challenging the night the western sky lights up
Thundering.

And all the sky is in a flare
With all the winds
And all the stars

Rushing...
And the rain
Swarming.

The moon
Mad queen of the earth,
Walks in the pools,

On the bridge's edge
The raindrops burst in spray
Dancing.

To the London Sparrow

Gamins.
Drab and
Cockney.
Wavering
but not much
between feeding and
...!

Thriftless.
Laying up children...
Dung growing less too.
What will become of you.
Your four broods yearly...
(or is it oftener.)

Will you go back to the country...
Corrupt poor relations....

Vibro-Massage

Moist warm towels
at my face
smell queerly...
chill me....

I am afraid....

...Unguents
smoothed into my face
like yellow silk
over my forehead.
...smoothed into cheek
into hollow.

Spasm...
Stress...
Pain...
Pressure
of keen sweet tears
from the lachrymals.

Brows
Nose
Cheek
Chin
exploring...
murmuring...
pulsing....

Body waiting...
yearning...
dreading....

Again...

Ecstatic...
Eyes shut,
Body shut,
Muscles tense,
Ecstasy
like a kiss...
the touch of hated hands....

Moist warm towels
at my face
smell queerly...
chill me....

Cold wet towels burn me...
their smell of death.

The Pub

How long, how very long have I been sitting here.
Tongue-tied and fixed within this murmuring stability.
Gaunt and immutable — through eyes that see not
Dim faces watch me.

The automatic piano plays and plays —
I grow sick, with anguish at the heart.
The piano thumps, skirls, goes out.

I fumble for a penny —
More music...
And again I grow sick.

Huge jewels glow behind the counter
Where the light comes through full bottles.

And still they urge me 'Drink.'
While the black-stoled murmurous figures
Dole the pain
At jingle of the coins.

Why does the barmaid there drink stout
Furtively.
Surely her breasts are big enough.

The After-Dinner Hooter

Peace.

A voice

Raucous, distensive,
Shatters and smashes
Concentrical.
Undermining
Unto the dimmest
Furthest proliferance
Of this pale whiteness.

Shivers the sphere... jangling.

Peace... trembling...
Still, still... be still!
Jangling, shivering... trembling.

Voices.

Shatters the sphere... jarring,
Bursting, jarring, bursting...
Still! still! Be still...
Ah...! shivering, BURSTING.

Item

To Margaret Drew

You said
your heart was
pieces of
                          strings

in a
peacock blue satin
                          bag.

London Night

Introduction. Still the void turns...
And creaks...
And spatters me...
With spume of gaunt fatuity...
And again turns...
Unceasingly...
Till the quiet burns.

The night is full, with laughter in its wings
(And faint wan faces ouched in yearning sky)
Laughter that weals the face of night... and stings...
The anguished soul drifts by.

I will not go...

Still the void turns...
And sickening thuds...
Creaking...
Still the quiet burns...
With flame that floods
The secret inner sky...
And yearns to the sound
And to the laughter...
I am called.
Hesitant,...

Still the void turns....

In the bus.   Hum of the town...
Splashes of faces
In garish places
Drive ever down....

In the Park.   The gaunt trees grope to the night.
The distant magic of the night...
And touch the sky...
The faces linger to the light
And endlessly drift by...
With shuffle of far feet like leaves that strike
And flicker on the way...
With little ripples of dry sound....

The band.   Noise of the band... and the wind asleep...
Over the wind I mount on wings
And swing and gleam and sheer and float....

How chill it is grown... and how remote the faces
And thin and very faint.... And the wind sings....

Interlude.   Shop girl, poor clerk
Ephemerons... wing your swift way
A little love — it will not mark
The soul unused to day...
So cold, so far away you seem
Shop girl... poor clerk....

I am the dreamer.... Are you the dream?

How the noise mocks me.... And the pain!

And they laugh about me.... While the
     trees unheard...
Though not to one or three the water calls in vain.
But only as an inner word...
For she is much more amorous then —
And will not prize her sweets too dear...
(For after all we are poor men
And may not know love... though here...)

18

Hyde Park Corner.	Stress of the crowd... And the whole of it mute... Tunics that thrill in the light... till you look at his face With a rush of hate... and hate for the grace Of the 'slavey' wooing the brute.

Stress of the crowd....

Picture Palace.	Breathless... The giggles cease... The ruddled alcove wafts me peace... And the clicking of the reel... Flicker of light... We thrill to the rush and the clatter... and spatter The night with our souls and... steal The soul of night... The girl at the box was very sweet... Manicured nails, and massaged smile, and teeth Resplendent... Flicker of light... The rush and the clatter... With that dust of fatuity Spattered... out of the void....

Always the streets and the giggle of girls
Women from where? God! but the night must be full
     of them....

Anarchist Club.	Quiet at last... she there... The babble of hot voices strangely soothes... The coffee is black... Avernus' waters where The soul's disquiets flare... And she... Her face like the halfold ivory A something past its whiteness... And cheeks ahollow.... Smoking ever talks she And disdains me quite. Not this the place. Later perhaps she will not say me nay... And ever and anon someone will say 'A bas' and 'saboter'.

How came we here?

Café	The sybaritic waiter brings us drink.... Thick lips and mottled face... ... I think His eyes go back to ancient arcadies... in the black Secret eyes of her... She is the beauty at the feast... My friends and their friend flock With words well greased...

19

Very fluent when the ideas flow...
Oh! but the babble wearies me
And the lights...
And rococo....

Liqueur.

One lotus bud swings to the harbour of my soul
And bursts...
And all its mystic whole
And each glad petal...thirsts
Unto all heaven...far roots
Insinuating...
Wondrous fruits
Creating.
Becoming of all things...
And God is singing...
Such a little song....

My moon, my almond-eyed delight goes from me
And I am old...
I am far older than she is...
And now she laughs at my grey hairs...
Yet may I not put forth to chasten her...
Lest she rebel...
I will use songs and fair words
To call her to my couch....

Then she shall languish forever
In the prison of my 'infinite mercy'.

Night....
I   am   afraid.

The Descent into Hell

A million years has passed.

Woven from many glooms
Out of many glooms
Into many glooms
I was.
I   and yet
Not I.

From the light
Woven into the dark.
Part... and not part.

Woven into the dark.
Part and not part
I am.

I was.

A million years pass.

Out of depths
Darkness draws me
Down stairs I do not see.
Each; white perfection of form.
And two steps wide.

Two steps wide....

I shall stumble if there are more stairs.

Two steps wide

Each their white perfection of form.

A million years pass.

With naked feet I will walk these stairs...
Caress their perfection...
The way will be shorter

Each their white perfection of form...
Horrible....

A million years pass.

I will walk naked
For any coolness that may be...

Many years pass.

There is no coolness.

A million years pass.	I will cast off this mind That whatever tremor there may be Must stir me....
A million years pass.	Nothing... White perfection Black and immobile Fills me....
A million years pass.	I will think on life.
Many, many years pass.	Each stair In white perfection of form Black and dead Draws me.
A million years pass.	I am not tired.
A million years pass.	But
Many years pass...	Down!
Many years pass...	Down...
Many years pass...	Down?
	Woven into the dark I... and yet Not I, Am... Was...
Many years pass.	Was?
Many, many years pass.	Am?

THEATRE MUET

1. Fear

A large room. At back the wall is semi-transparent, and dimly through this the wall of the opposite corridor may be seen. A figure passing down this corridor would appear shadowy and in silhouette. Everything in the room is very clear in the strong light of a hot summer afternoon. There is a door, back left corner.

Pierrot and Columbine play chess.
They play in silence for many seconds.
Then steps are heard. They commence in the upper parts of the house, moving slowly down a corridor, and very deliberately descending the stairs until they reach the door of the room.
Nobody.
The corridor remains empty.
Pierrot goes to the door, which he opens casually, glances out and seeing nothing, returns to the chessmen. Columbine has sat quietly watching the game.
Again steps are heard.
Pierrot hears them while they are still in the upper part of the house; listening intently as they descend the stairs. He rushes to the door, fumbling at the handle. The steps fade away.
Again he returns to the table.
Columbine trembles when a pawn is put down.
The steps recommence, slowly and very deliberately.
When they reach the door Pierrot flings it open.
Nothing!
Columbine stands trembling.
Both wait behind the door (now open) trembling.
Again the steps are heard descending, but slyly and maliciously, and lingering as though familiarly on the boards till they reach them.
Nothing.
And they tremble.
Wearily they return to the chessboard.
They hear suddenly two short steps and a tap at the door.
Pierrot rushes to the door.
Columbine has risen. Suddenly she starts as though touched — and again — and again. She begins weeping, but no sound is heard.
The steps, deliberate and very clear, recommence in the upper corridor.
Pierrot returns to the chess.
The steps are not heard.
They recommence playing, often starting as the pieces touch the board.
The steps are heard.
Pierrot rushes from the room. His figure is silhouetted vaguely through the semi-transparent wall as he rushes to and fro. Twilight is in the room.
Columbine stands still.

Suddenly she turns as though touched by someone — and again — and again. Unable to bear the strain she rushes after Pierrot.

Two pairs of feet are heard running through the upper parts of the house. A door slams.

Occasionally they re-pass each other behind the semi-transparent wall, but as though oblivious of each other, stopping and turning often; bewildered.

They are heard mounting stairs.

The rushing of feet grows fainter, louder, fainter.

Sometimes a third pair of feet seem to be echoing them, sometimes distinct, sometimes mere echo.

Then they seem to be playing, softly and slyly and maliciously, moving over the boards, and after them the feet of Pierrot and Columbine.

In the corridor, behind the semi-transparent wall, Pierrot and Columbine run wildly past each other, to and fro, to and fro.

Sometimes it seems there is another form, more tenuous still, moving with them, in and out, in and out; disappearing sometimes. They are heard mounting stairs. Two pairs of feet, loudly and hurriedly, and after them, softly and slyly and maliciously, a third.

Very suddenly; deep silence.

Night.

2. The Lunatic

Columbine is seated on a kitchen chair before a wide French window, which looks on to a terrace overhanging the edge of the world. The room is very large, but the wallpaper is drab, like a slum room. In a corner is an iron bedstead covered with very white blankets. It is a warm night.

The moon can be seen rising.

Columbine sits still, relaxed and brooding.

The rising moon touches her naked arms.

She looks round, startled and shivering.

Then folds her arms over her breast.

Then rises and walks in front of the window in extreme agitation.

After a while she grows calmer and returns to the chair, seating herself.

She remains quiet a few moments, but the moonbeams pierce her.

They shine on her bare arms.

She trembles, raising them and looking at them curiously ... and lifts them slowly, suddenly kissing them.

Then falls a-trembling.

She rises and walks up and down in great agitation.

When she grows quieter, she returns to her chair.

The moonbeams fall full on her and again she raises her arms to her lips, kissing them.

She folds her arms tightly across her breast, rocking herself.
She opens the window wide, leaning out as though exhausted.
The moonbeams strike her. She becomes very excited.
She walks in front of the window to and fro.
Then seats herself on the chair.
The moonbeams are in another corner of the room, and she sits relaxed and brooding.

3.   Twilight

I

Columbine, Harlequin, and Pierrot sit relaxed in armchairs in a wide, white room.

Columbine sits swinging her legs.
It grows gradually darker.
They sit as though waiting.
Creepers swing against the window.
It grows darker.
They sit as though waiting.
It grows darker.
Only the windows and the white linen of Pierrot and Columbine can now be seen.
Harlequin a faint blur.
It grows darker.
Pierrot and Columbine show faintly. The easy-chairs are rocks of shadow.
They sit as though waiting. . . .
The creepers grow larger and swing against the windows.
It grows darker.

4.   Twilight

II

Columbine, Harlequin, and Pierrot sit relaxed in easy-chairs in a wide, white room.

They sit as though waiting.
It grows darker. . . .
The moon rises.
They sit as though waiting.
It is quite dark.
Columbine shudders, rises and walks quickly to Pierrot.

When she is close she turns from him suddenly and walks rapidly back to her chair. . . .

Harlequin leaps across the room, then seats himself and stares intently out of the window.

The moon gradually fills the room and it becomes lighter.

Pierrot has let his head fall on his knees.

Columbine sits relaxed swinging her legs. . . .

Harlequin stares intently out of window.

5.   Interior

Black Curtain.

In one corner the picture of a door.

A man in black tights (so that only his face is seen and the outlines of his body divined) crosses the stage.

He passes through the door.

We follow him because the curtain is raised.

Black room.

Again he crosses the stage and striking a match, lights a gas jet at his own height with great deliberation.

Man goes off unseen.

Three chairs become apparent.

They are in a line — two kitchen chairs —
once white — dirty.

One — old — beautiful —
highly polished.

In the flickering light the three chairs grow
unutterably mournful.

6.   The End of the World

Amphitheatre.

Dawn. Cold very cold.

Men and women in evening dress move over the floor of the amphitheatre.

Grouping — regrouping.

Wandering distraught like those damned souls in halls of Eblis.

They form and reform groups.

Dawn — and it is cold — very cold.

Then a whispering wakes among them and it is the restless stirring of dead leaves.

Let us go home — they say — each to the other — wandering distraught like damned souls in halls of Eblis.

Let us go home — and it is the stirring of dead leaves

Let us go home.

7.   Hunger

The Celestial Quire.

The lambent sea-green flames that are the celestial quire burn shrilly, striving. . . .

They describe the circle which is Kosmos, swirling shrilly.

When they writhe it is outside three-dimensioned space.

Forever they return in their orbits.

Forever they return in their orbits.

If they writhe at all, it is outside the three-dimensioned spaces.

They do not touch each other. They do not clash with each other.

Nor is there light in Space.

8.

A room. Sombre faces of 1, 2, and 4 (women) in profile.

Man (3) with back to audience.

They are seated round a gas fire.

Glow seen through legs and chair legs.

A silent duel in progress between 1 and 3 seated diagonally.

2 and 4, more or less neutral, obscure issue.

Conversation clockwise (need not be materialised).

1. 'What shall it be then, Cerise?'
2. 'It was a lovely party.'
2. 'Pouf' (lights a cigarette).
4. Sighs (blow out smoke).

Silence.

Conversation resumed. Same things more or less. The man's back becomes inimical, hating 1. His back muscles prepare to spring and so ripple to crouch.

1 trembles, fearful. Tries to talk to show her nonchalance, fails. Her heart beats thud, thud, thud.

2 and 4 neutral, disturb inimic waves.

The man loses his tenseness. Obscurely he collects all his forces for a final overwhelming, but they dissipate among 2 and 4 (neutral). 4 now becomes sympathetic to him and so drains more vitality. 1 stiffens, gathers that 2 is her ally. Also 4 unconsciously.

Man rises to his feet. For a moment tries to gather vitality through firm feet and twitching fingers.

His shoulders fall, he stumbles out.

Three sighs of relief.

Conversation:
1. What shall it be?
2. Such a lot of men!

Hours later:
1 in bed. Mass of shadow on white sheets.
Cannot sleep, tosses about.
Attack of nerves.
One feels it has gone on for hours.
She seeks relief.

9.   To S.E.R.

Man and Woman, face to face. Same height. Woman facing audience.

Woman mad, breathing heavily, whites of eyes showing, striking man in face, once...twice.

His back is to audience. No muscle of it moves. (Inert — a crumbling block of salt).

Her madness drops. His passivity makes her doubt his reality — then her own.

In the uncertain pause, she is again assured of her reality.

More blows, same effects.

Tears blind her, she dashes them away.

More blows, face distorted.

Still same effects.

The ubiquitous man, appearing and reappearing (real and phantom) before her strained eyes makes them water.

She feels it a weakness — swallows. Another weakness.

Stares dully at the figure before her.

Impotence realised — weeps.

Weeps loudly and slobberingly and hopelessly like a whipped child.

Weeps more loudly yet, more hopelessly: with distorted muscles, copious tears and lengthening and coarsening of upper lip.

Such lack of control is intolerable.

Members of the audience want to strike each other.

<table>
<tr><td>Audience
Intellectual
and otherwise.</td><td>A few women weep too, in identical pitch.
It becomes a panic spreading suddenly.
The men leave quickly, swallowing hard.
One man throws a brickbat at the inert back, then another.
Others do the same.
When he sinks stoned, expiring — a yell of exultation rises from the men — long sighs of relief from the women.
'ANTICHRIST'</td></tr>
</table>

Outside the Theatre — weeping: fitful, intolerable — mounts from street to street and star to star in festoons of distinguished and unutterable melancholy.

10.

1.

Thick twilight. A long row of houses, several storeys high.

All have area railings and steps leading up to the front door.

One light in a top window a third of the way down the block.

A drab yellow light also works through glass of street door.

A woman walks (bent) on the pavement in front of these houses hovering undecidedly, evidently fearful.

Then she draws herself together and climbs the steps leading to the lit door.

She waits shuffling from foot to foot, seeming undecided — (she has rung the bell).

The door opens a little, a wedge of light moves out and a dark figure appears for a moment breaking it. They talk for a few seconds, and both enter. The door shuts. A wedge of darkness passes across the lit panes.

The light works out tranquilly again.

2.

Stairs dimly lit, narrow, carpeted. The figure climbs, climbs, climbs — foreboding, distrust and fear at every point.

3.

A room — walls dark red; small, stuffy, unbearable.

The woman stands uneasily just inside the door — waiting.

The room is full of impending tragedy.

Influences are in the room and in the next room.

Tragedy becomes apparent in the woman's pose.

She waits.

Nothing happens.

With dramatic suddenness, her body droops — she cringes.

(Nothing, nothing, NOTHING happens).

Curtain — very quietly, like a sigh, so that it is some seconds before audience realises that play is over.

11.   The Bowed Head

I see the bowed head silhouetted on air.

There pass in frieze behind her, wrack of civilisation, murder, rape, vast conflagration.

The breast hangs withered, rachitic childhren wail and are still.

The head is bowed.

Ten thousand young men are convulsed in death.

Ten thousand howl to writhing women.

They too are still.

The head is bowed.

Cold creeps from the stars.

Snow settles like a down.

Ice constrains earth powerfully and for ever —

I see the bowed head silhouetted on air.

12.

The curtain is raised upon Autumn and closely interwoven trees. Dead leaves in profusion. Behind is seen a long field with stocks of corn which mist is clotting.

Behind — mountains.

Curtain drops.

The curtain is raised again and a woman is standing beneath the trees, half in shadow. It is the first phase of twilight.

Evidently she is waiting.

The mist grows denser and gradually envelopes the trees so that the woman is blotted out.

The trees multiply rapidly; she is in a dense thicket (clearing disappears); the mist rises.

Steps are heard in the leaves — the trees dwindle; they become bushes.

The sky grows darker but clearer — the evening star ascends.

A man — and she rushes to meet him. Everything quickly blots out in curtain of black and yellow with spots and streaks that whirl excentrically as they embrace. This disappears as they draw apart. Trees gradually climb higher again and while they regard each other the landscape resumes its appearance as at the opening of the scene.

They approach and seize each other. The swirl of colour again appears but with the original landscape diminished upon it.

They separate.

They have become colossal in comparison with what is around them, but gradually as they are sucked into it the trees resume their normal size, the mist creeps out thickly.

It grows darker with more stars. The time for parting approaches.

The trees grow higher and higher, become a thick forest, very cold. The mist threads the trunks milkily.

It is evident he must go.

They embrace, and for a moment the trees seem to dwindle and then shoot up terrifically engulfing her. She cowers.

Rustling of leaves, — his receding footsteps.

THE DUTCH DOLLS

The Dutch Dolls

'Hi, Hi, Hi…' — Verlaine.

To young men, who, being loved, therefrom engender within them a true
passion, enduring nobly its heats and its chills and the vagaries of mistresses
under the phases of the moon.

Who, seeing each new incident with the most intimate and disillusioning
psychology, yet remain silent; and having suffered with what noble forbear-
ance, learn they are reviled therefor.

Gentlemen, The Dutch Dolls!

Pierrot

Tomorrow will pass like other days.
Fear, hate, anger,
and at times…
peace.
This till I'm with her.
Then pain, anger, contempt,
and in rare moments,
peace.

Through it all this pitiless unrest
will hold me fast,
till I must go
terrified and blank,
sombre like this street,
these lowering houses,
and she who watches
from trivial curtains
my footfalls sucked into eternity.

Her first love

Leaning over her while she lay
thrown back across my knees, …
I bruised her lips
and the small hard breasts
with strainings and caresses.

She does not move…
says nothing
Is she wondering what it all means?

But now and then her eyes water, their lids droop,
and her lips quiver.
Her face grows darker...
She strains me to her desperately...

It's hard to know what these young girls want!

Going home

Come with me to the station!
No!
You don't love me.
Oh...
Come then!
'When you go I want to cry.'
His own eyes watered, and he felt for the handle of the door.
How empty the room would be when he'd gone.
The idea oppressed him.
A wild straining each to each.
Don't go!
He freed himself
Ah, No! No!
But he said sadly, you can't keep me.
She went out of the room with averted head.

He knew her eyes would follow him down the street, but he did
    not look back at the window.
She might wave to him... who left her thus forever —
Forever...
Ah... till tomorrow.

Backtalk

It's you, I love, only you!
What then?
You, you, only you!
As much as other men.
You, you, only you!
Come then!
You, you, ah... as much as other men.

The Moonmaiden

Come!
No!
I will give you a white horse.
No!
I will give you a white baby.
No!
I will give you a white house.
No!
I will give you my own white dead body.
No! it's cold, get my cloak.
 . . . . . .

Damn you, Columbine.
Then they didn't 'core you.

      (She weeps.)

Interlude — Nostalgie de l'infini

You tangoed with him
on the lawn
in the moon,
and I smiled.

At times you'd be strong,
walk to me.
You did not think I shook;
hated you.

And when you'd dance with me,
I went away.

Why do you tell me these years after,
you wept for a long night?

The plot thickens

I laid upon my love
the spell of the kiss,
and left her to her bitter pain.

Outside was Carnival.

When I returned
she was gone.
The night was cold
but I slept warm,
for I said
she sleeps more cold than I.

That my love should leave me
hurts me nothing;
But that the spell of my kiss
might thus easily be broken,
I am ashamed.

The Emperor's Nightingale

It's only you, I love
she says,
and cannot say aught else.
Poor 'Emperor's nightingale'.

You, you, ah you,
she sighs.

But yet, when I 'go off',
she'll fling her kisses
for all the gallery to snarl upon,
And so 'come off'
and rapt
will pass me on the stairs.

Celtic!

We danced, poor fools, on the world's edge.

Because I saw her nimble legs
clean against the sky,
now there is no thing will give me ease.

I'll find again that edge of the world
whereon she dances.

Poor fool! she dances on the world's edge.

The compassionate pilgrim

I laughed,
chatted gaily;
was most attentive
to the foil I'd brought to pique you.
You'd no notion.

And though you laughed,
I saw through it
and was not hurt.

After,
you stood silent, lone
most pitiful.

All this trouble
because I could not kiss you
in the crowded room.

You wanted to keep me
But they'd not let you,
and you gave way.
Now I'm gone
and you're a memory.
Silent, lone,
most pitiful.

The Betrayal

This face is mine,
Hollow and line.
The same, yet bitter wine
I'm drunk upon.

T'was held by one
Who falsely spun
A web of love,
Below, above.

Yet it will prove
Her evil, should she turn,
But see the lips agirn,
Sad eyes, that burn, that burn.

Excuses himself for being concerned at her going.

I've written enough to you,
about you
and because of you;
and dragged your beauty into too much light.

Now I'll nurse an aching heart
and with no outlet for the pain
will crush it under.
I'll forget you in a while
remembering you're nothing.

When I was young,
child of the sun,
imminent with fire
I did not write of women.

But you have taken the ichor from my veins,
You have watered the vitriol of my brain.

Day-Dreamings

You'll be sorry later on —
for I'll come back
and, chancing on you in some public place,
you'll tremble. I'll be bronzed;
contempt upon my face;
ah...not for you,
only that I'll have seen strong men dying.
She that's fairest will be on my arm
and in my pocket a thousand pounds.

You'll laugh...
in spasms of fear...your eyes will go blank...
and I'll not sleep for thinking of you
wide-eyed at his side.

In Defence

If I'd not burnt your letters as they came
for fear their weight of love would stifle me,
for fear when I'd grown old
my children or my love would find them,
or older still
the pitiful scrawl across the pages
would mad me with the longing —
... all the pain of youth that passes...
Would I have thus forgot them all —
remembering the half of a phrase,
the splash of a tear.

But you kept my letters
and those I wrote most passionate
when I had ceased to love you,
you showed most proudly.

Therefore your friends think
'Poets' oh they're but human
to let themselves be scorned so by mere woman.

Columbine becomes advanced

I hate you!
Kiss me!
Now I really hate you!
Kiss me! There... you see.

Oh... how I hate you now.

You're dull, Columbine,
Good Night!

[Part II]

Ah, Columbine!
It's here my tragedy begins:
for I could eat my heart out in these poems;
hating you, despising you, despairing of you.

And all this then to count for nothing;
you not to recall these poems when you see them printed,
for they'll be vague to you
as they are now to me.
And t'will be other women weeping, reading them
will think
'I'd not have spoiled things so.'

Only... I've got you fast,
I taught you love
and all the learning I put in that
I've so put in these poems,
that I've you fast for ever.
While I've them I've you
and when and where I call
you'll come, you can't but come!
But just now you may go
I've other things and do not want you.

Still... be happy.
I'll want you yet —
and would not want you crabbed.

Unliterary

Your tears were nothing to me;
nor any woman's tears.
The tears of dead queens
move me profoundly.

You know, after a month or so of spooning
I got rather tired of it all.
Your tears were nothing to me.

Do you remember our walk in the wood?
we quarrelled:

44

and I remembered the 'Poèmes Saturniens'
in my pocket.

And when I read to myself
'Je fais souvent ce rêve',
and you were outside it all...
you were humiliated.

I think now I was needlessly cruel.
Your tears were nothing to me.

[*Untitled*]
I dislike you when you dance
when all your body shows out obvious,
your flat feet
and the gold hair gray in the limes.

You will not know I ever hated you,
and still you'll say —
Do you love me?
and I'll say Yes! and ah... and
Do you love me?
till you say oh...
and cling and cling.
And when you've had your fill of me
I'll go away and hate you
till you come murmuring
Poor fellow! he's sick for love of me.
Perhaps it's true.

Time's Healing

Dear love, because I hated you,
I vulgarized you, loosed your belt —
and not content with that —
defiled your modesty
by flinging the secret ways of your mind
to lecherous satyrs.
Yet — I'd not undo it.

Ah, if I could write a white poem
like 'La Jeune Fille un peu souffrante'
I'd think myself a 'poet'.

I must feed on my heart's blood,
madness plunged in the throbbing of my brain,
my vision swam. . . hands failed
when I wrote down these poems —
and now I do not know why they were printed.

To prove that I was a god, or you were a god,
that I was a worm, or you were a worm,
or clever — or clear psychologists —
or perhaps to show it was play or something more serious,
or to clear myself in my wife's eyes,
or to show that I always hated you or always loved you,
or that you were everything to me — or nothing?

The Serpent

You sly little devil
what do you take me for?

And if I do frivol at love with you
and it pleases me
gives me a new interest
still you mustn't do that!

You should be madly in love
a real 'grande passion'
(first or later doesn't much matter
women always take love seriously)
your letters should be half-unreadable
with all the tear stains.

I'd be worried rather, rather pleased
by such a strong love,
and wonder anxiously,
how it's all to end.

But you're   playing too
you sly little devil.

Finis!

Having raised her to the highest place: —
Flung power, glory, wisdom at her feet,
we drive her higher yet, to meet
Man — lord of light, all glory and all grace.

And we have crowned her in the sacred fane,
where sole the earth-purged arts may strain.

Damn that girl! she's on her back again.

Envoi to Columbine

I'm changed
I saw you yesterday
pink-eyed, pale cheeked,
with scanty eyebrows:
Poor you, poor me
that can no longer love you.
And if you're happy or sad
what is it now to me?

In past days
I thought I'd put you by
till that time I should want you.
(You'll say twas you who jilted me)
but now I do not want you.

Are you happy, sad —
what is it now to him
who does not want you,
save for a half regret that Time
has played him this sad trick.

SKETCHES AND PROSE POEMS

Three Nightpieces

Toward eight o'clock I begin to feel my pulses accelerating quietly. A little after, my heart begins to thump against its walls. I tremble all over, and leaving the room rapidly go out on the terrace of the house and look over the weald.

There is a shadowiness of outline and the air is crisp. The sky in one corner is a pale nostalgic rose. The trees look like weeds and a bird flies up through them like a fish lazily rising. The hills really look like breasts: and each moment I look for the head of the Titan negress to rise with the moon in the lobe of her ear.

I think of my youth and the intolerable legacy it left me.

I think of the crazy scaffolding of my youth and wonder why I should be surprised that the superstructure should be crazy too, wavering to every breeze and threatening ever to come down about my ears. I think too of wrongs done to this one and that one, and... 'Oh, my God,' I cry, 'I did not know, I did not know,' and my heart thumps louder in my breast and my pulses throb like a tide thundering and sucking at some crumbling jetty.

I gulp deep breaths of air to steady myself, but it is of no good. I think of her whom I love and futility overwhelms me: for this too will have its common end, and our orbits grow ever remoter. And putting my head on my breast, faint and reminiscent — the smell from my armpits rises to my brain, and she stands before me vividly and the same smell comes from her; but it is more heady and more musky and she looks at me with intolerable humility.

And a minute after there is only the dark; a hoot-owl's terrifying call and the queer yap that comes in reply; the frogs that thud through the grass like uncertain feet; the trees that talk to each other.

And I would willingly let my life out gurgling and sticky, and sink without a bubble into its metallic opacity.

II

I had gone to bed quietly at my wife's side, kissing her casually as was my custom. I awoke about two in the morning with a start so sudden that it seemed I had been shot by a cannon out of the obscurity of sleep into the light of waking; at one moment I had been, as it were, gagged and bound by sleep; and the next I was wide awake and could distinctly sense the demarking line between sleep and waking. And this demarking line was like a rope made of human hair such as one sees in exhibitions of indigenous Japanese products.

In my ears still rang the after-waves of the shriek which had awakened me. The nerves governing my skin were still out of control as a result of the sudden fright, and portions of it continued twitching for a long time after; my scalp grew cold in patches and my hair stood on end.... In the dark

I found myself trembling all over and bathed in a cold sweat. . . . And it was impossible to collect myself. My wife, I felt, was sitting up in bed and a minute afterward she began to weep quietly.

I was still trembling and her quiet weeping made me more afraid. I was angry with her too, but could not talk to her, I was so afraid. My voice, I knew, would have issued thin and quavering, and I was afraid of its hollow reverberations losing themselves uncertainly in the darkness. By the little light I saw her put her hands up to her head in despair . . . as though still half asleep; and before I could stop her again the same piercing, incredibly terrifying shriek burst from her. Again I trembled all over, involuntarily gnashing my teeth and feeling my skin ripple like loathsome worms.

'Stop,' I cried, seizing her by the arms, 'Stop,' afraid to wake her, yet more afraid to hear again that appalling shriek — and in a moment she was awake . . . looking wildly round her, and the quiet weeping gave way to a wild and tempestuous sobbing.

I was afraid of her, afraid to go on sleeping with her, lest she should again shriek in that wild and unearthly fashion; afraid to fall asleep again lest I should be awakened by that appalling shriek dinning in my ears and my body quivering vilely under the impossible sound. I clung to her: 'What is it, tell me at least what it is,' I said.

For a time she would not tell me. Trembling all over with anguish and fear of I knew not what, I insisted. When at last she did tell me it was as though the world had suddenly been cut away from under my feet. Helplessly and weeping I clung to her, with cold at my heart. That any human being could accuse another of devilry so sinister, so cold, so incredible even in dream, I had not conceived of. Loathing her, I clung the closer in my anguish and despair.

III

One night at supper I had eaten cucumber. Soon after I went to bed and on the first strokes of ten fell asleep.

After sleeping for a long time I awoke into a dimly lit room. I still lay on the bed and after a moment a figure entered, and after a few moments more, another, until in this fashion there were half a dozen people in the room. I could not distinguish who they were, and quietly and obscurely they moved round my bed. Now and then there was a hiss out of the corners of the room, or a chuckle in reply to some unheard obscenity.

A heavy weight oppressed me as though I knew they menaced me in some obscure and dreadful way. I could not move.

I could not move, and always the same obscure and dreadful procession encircled me and shadowy bodies pressed a little closer, then drew back again to join the sinister group.

And though I saw nothing save their shadowy forms, I knew their eyes gleamed down at me: their faces were lecherous: their hands clawed; and forever and through long ages they went round me in sinister procession.

Suddenly... and how I do not know, I had broken the bonds of sleep and lay trembling in a cold sweat. Through my protecting blankets the last strokes of ten were fading.

Possession

I never willingly entered that room after twilight, unless someone had first lit the gas. If I needed something badly from that room, I sent someone else. If there was no one else it took me five minutes to screw up courage.

I waited outside the door with fingers on handle. A quiver of awakening life seemed to come through the wood. The room was awaiting me.

I waited. The expectation behind the door seemed to have died down. The room no doubt thought I had changed my mind. I laughed, flinging open the door quickly.

Once inside fear dropped from me. I too became part of the room. That part of my brain which before had leapt in fear now beat casually. My mind became blank. I had forgotten what it was I came for. I took a chair — and walking on my toes carried it to the window. The room was filled with grey twilight. Reflection from the polished surfaces of furniture looked like bars of silver laid across sideboard and table. The green carpet was lost in a pit of darkness.

Everything in the room waited. The chairs; and with white glassy stare the pictures; a tense eager waiting as though they held their breaths.

I too waited, looking through the window. Down the narrow street lights sprang suddenly into opposite windows and the street was so narrow that opposite roofs hung over me like an immense bluff, between us an incredible precipice I sat on, waiting.

Suddenly my heart would seem to stop, my body fall to ground with a sudden and dreadful crash; and my wife would be by my side, tearful and excited 'I've been looking for you all over the house.'

Incidents in the Life of a Poet

At seventeen he had made up his mind that Fate had destined him for a high sphere, yet how inexpressibly sordid Life was. He became a philosophical anarchist. Later, when he found that Shelley too had been an anarchist, his pride knew no bounds. Then the greatness of his destiny made it impossible to risk it by throwing bombs. Nevertheless he was convinced that bomb-throwing was the only panacea.

Fortunately for his self-respect he remembered that 'The pen is mightier than the sword'.

*

At eighteen he was embarrassed by the frequency with which middle-aged women fell on his neck, hailing him as the poetical genius of the future. He began to take it for granted. Therefore he cut his hair; wore a bowler; did his utmost in fact to look like a stockbroker and man of spirit; for he thought — 'since the greatness of my future is so certain, why waste energy in trying to look it. Besides what is more intriguing than a dark horse?'

Alas, the very women who had been the first to tell him of his divine mission, now spurned him. 'We were mistaken,' they said to each other; 'After all, he has the mind of a stockbroker!'

*

At nineteen he was surprised by the frequency with which young women fell in love with him. Not because he was a man — nor even because of his art — but because, 'he looked so girlish', they said.

'Was it' he could not refrain from asking himself, 'a refined form of Lesbianism?' His whole soul revolted at the idea.

He spent long hours pushing his chin forward: he got drunk quite frequently: he became a specialist in bawdy-houses.

He adopted a brutal and incisive form of speech with these women: and allowed no subject to be taboo in discussion.

Alas, they were only the more convinced of his profound femininity.

It was exactly the way they talked to each other.

*

Strangely enough, although his poetry was of heroic mould, he was a coward. The idea of physical injury made him sick and he could not bear to tread on a worm. (No, dear reader, he was not such a coward as to be afraid of it turning.) If he passed over a bridge where children were playing, his heart would stop beating and his knees liquefy under him at the thought that one of them would fall in, in which case he would have to dive the hundred feet or so into the water; perhaps get wet — even perhaps a cold, — risk his destiny for the sake of a slum brat: for unfortunately he could swim and dive too, but not very well.

One day at Margate (he was a poet whose destiny was to describe the life of his time), he had finished bathing and was in his machine looking out to sea. He saw a girl and a man swim out, with a tide strongly running. Then the man turned back and the girl threw up an arm, and cried 'Help'. He was scandalised to see that the man had left her and that no one else went in. Feeling the world to be full of injustice he realised that after all he would have to go in. He dropped into the water casually — first putting on his wet costume (les convenances must be observed) — and pulled her out. He had to sweat over it, but managed it finally by swimming obliquely against the tide.

Both collapsed on the beach. Then the girl murmured 'Thank you', and disappeared. The crowd cheered. He went into his tent. He realised now how heroes were made, quite casually, just like that. He dressed himself, and after a proper interval left the machine proudly as befitted a hero; prepared to receive the acclamation, — perhaps even a collection — from the crowd who had witnessed the deed. At least, he thought, my photograph in the *Mirror* ought to sell out those damned sonnets. And the girl — ah the girl — she would surely be waiting to throw her arms round his neck and be his bride.

There was nobody on the beach — he looked on every hand — not even a Mystic Choir anywhere. And the thin clapping of dead leaves mocked him.

*

Of course he was in love: quite often in fact. Each new woman was that one for which his whole soul had longed. She alone was the one vision who had solaced his sleepless nights, visiting him in dreams. Never was poet so rhapsodical, never woman so idolised — never union more inspiring.

Alas, soon she began to cry 'Give me bread, meat, children.' He was, of course, penniless.

There was the usual scene. She said he had no right to be a poet without a rich father behind him. It was directly contrary to Novelette precedent. What about Shelley, etc.

'I can't live on air, if you *can!*' She slammed the front door.

When he was thus deserted, he would question himself: 'Am I unhappy?' Yes, there was no use denying it, he was. 'Joy' he cried, 'for only through suffering shall one gain eternal life', i.e. write eternal poetry.

While he wrote the sonnet inspired by the above, he was already seeing how it would go to the Editor. The postman would throw it into the 'sanctum' with a pile of other letters. He pictured the Editor's amazement, when he opened his sonnet, read his letter, and how he would admire the dignity of the covering letter. 'Dear Sir, herewith I beg to enclose you a sonnet which you may care to print. I am, Sir, etc.' Here was the poet for whom the Editor had sought so long. He would rush out, hail a taxi, dash up to the poet's door, take him home and give him a square meal at last; buy all his other stuff at incredible sums a line.

Alas, his father died before ever he had a sonnet accepted, and he had put £2000 into the dying *Réclame* first. Therefore the sonnet appeared in *The Réclame*.

※

One day he was in a bad mood. His anger grew with every word of the story he was telling to his large friend.

' "So then," she said, "do you like my new frock?"

' "Admirable", I said.

' "And do you love me better in it?"

' "No", I said, thinking of the sonnets she'd promised to print with the money, "I think it's a nice frock, but not more pleasant than your other frocks, or no frock at all for that matter. One knows of course that people must have frocks sometimes."

' "Yes," she said. "I simply had to. Just as sometimes I have to have smart hats, — just as I have to have you. They're all just as necessary to me as each other. Sometimes my only desire is a hat, or else it's a box at the theatre, or else it's a frock — or else —" and then she beamed at me — "it's you." '

There was a ferocious silence which irked the friend, and to break it he said 'Well, what did you say to that?'

'Say? I strangled her.'

※

At twenty-one he decided the time had come for his Magnum Opus. It was to be a novel. At last the human soul would be torn bare, — disclosed in all its innate vileness and nobility.

With the object of unveiling Isis, he therefore said to his sweetheart: 'Darling, there must have been times when you hated me; when you felt you'd burst if you had to see me ever again; and all because of things I had done unwittingly and which offended you the more because of it. It's no good denying it, because it always happens in love.'

'Yes, all right' she said. 'But you tell me yours first.'

'No, you first' he said.

'No you! then I promise I will.'

'No you' he replied, 'then I will.'

'What must his thoughts have been like,' she thought, 'since he's so ashamed to own them'; and left him there and then and forever.

※

At the age of twenty-five he had written, in chronological order, a volume of sonnets, a novel, a play; believe me, all showing marked talent. Then his father providentially died. His first thought was to forswear the Muses. When he entertained old friends he took care to wear with his newly-acquired velvet dinner jacket an air of ferocious melancholy.

'Well, what are you writing now, John?' they would ask.

'Nothing' he would reply shortly. 'What's the good of the damned game, I want to know? All dust and ashes. In a hundred years where is it all? No! I'm going abroad. I mean to have a good time — wine, women and song. I've talked about it long enough, heaven knows. The only thing that kept me at it in the old days was the thought that the old man would go on till I was fifty or so and I'd have to keep going somehow.'

When they had gone he remained in thought. An insidious voice whispered in his ear 'That little scene now would make a good prose-poem. Not for publication, of course, but just interesting. It wouldn't take you a few minutes. Just the poet — now wealthy — literature forsworn for ever and ever, stretching out his hand to a sheet of paper.'

'What an old hypocrite you are, John', he said as he went into the library.

*

When his father died he went abroad.

His destiny went with him and gave him no rest.

Then he thought 'Even if I rescue my name from oblivion for a hundred years only, it would have been worth while.'

A hundred years — why the mere fact of printing a book gains it admission to the British Museum Library. Surely that institution must last as long as the British Empire, i.e. for ever and ever —

So then, it would be quite a simple matter to last as long as any of the classics in that superb library.

He decided that the means of lasting to Eternity were too simple, too easily procured for one of so electric a mind as himself.

It was like preserving coprolites.

He was glad he could afford to forgo Literature.

Theseus

When the brass door of the labyrinth clanged behind him he was in darkness. The noise reverberated in his ears and grew fainter, like an omen called from hill-top to hill-top till it died ten thousand miles into the heart of a continent. He waited for the last echo to fade; for the hollow sound lay about him like a wild beast's eyes. But however faint and ultimate the hullo-ing grew, always further and fainter and more ominous, another echo woke. He waited an eternity. The last remote vibration died. He put one foot forward: stealthily and so faintly that an effort to strain his ears to catch the sound, seemed to burst a blood-vessel deep in his brain; another echo awoke. He could not stand it. 'Haia' he shouted into the dark, 'Haia': determined to kill forever that globular and staring echo. The sound went crashing along the dark galleries, and came spitting and crashing back to him like thunder, and ready to bring the walls down about him.

He was afraid and lifted his shield above his head.

'Mother', he cried, instinctively.

He began to go forward. His feet made no sound: he could see nothing. When he touched the wall he drew his hand away: it was wet and slimy and felt like a snake's skin. Sometimes he turned right-angles, following the walls. It did not matter.

He tried not to think of the approaching encounter, so that he might reserve his strength, but in its place he only saw Ariadne whom he hated. He tried to think of the girl he had left behind, but her face had grown vague and her eyes ghostly.

Still he marched on. At first he had walked warily, dreading surprise at each moment, but as he saw that the corridors were only a man's breadth he regained confidence.

He walked till each step had become automatic. He had forgotten whether he walked or not. Only if he stopped could he know, but this did not occur to him.

A sudden turn brought him up sharp, and he stopped. The muscles of his legs and calves began to twitch spasmodically and with excruciating pain. He was forced to go on.

Still the dark held, and though he strained his eyes to see what lay before him, he only saw lines of white fire darting across his sight, and these burst with a little splatter when they reached the edge of his retina.

At first he thought he was seeing light: then he knew that the gods were laughing at him.

He saw pale outlines of a stomach appear on the dark before him, and it was like a drawing on a slate. He knew by that he was hungry.

His bowels began to gripe, calling for food, and the peristalt drew for him a figure 8, with the long axis lying horizontal. The motion of each foot as it touched ground translated itself into a circle of fire, flashing first on one side of his brain and then on the other.

He did not know if he walked or not. He felt his eyes bursting from his head. Purkinje's figures danced before him, making a pink haze. There was a little tug behind him — and a cord snapped.

Dancer

Gyroscope hums immutably through buttocks — threatens and terrifies — pervading obscure oscillation. A world set into motion, uncontrollable.

But in opposite direction and actually and with a more furious obscurity of oscillation hips burn with more febrile and human life. Then the shoulders — and, moving down like a snake, the ribs prepare for action. Furiously the head gyrates, veers — a synthetic five moon of Saturn. Thighs and legs are pivotted on quicksilver — they cannot give — head and buttocks dangle from Sirius.

Buttocks sway alternately — a floating pier — one is terrified lest they break away, continue their ponderous flight, through a space where there is no darkness, for we are atoms glued to their axes.

Neck and head joggle like five mad moons in steel blue. But from the bulb one yellow shaft swerves out — blinding. The machine clanks — shivers on quicksilver, a surface cut to files by winds denser than metals — but the gravid beauty totters, then stands, for quintessential concentrations jab one from the heel.

The trunk twists like a reed upon the sinister lake of dynamism made by buttocks — yet revolves about them. From each heel the marvellous upthrust makes the buttocks topple from one side of the strut to the other.

Machine accreted from birth, oiled much. Such a belly — tight like a drum.

One hundred rotations in as many planes.

Buttocks strutted recklessly, firm against quicksilver, heeling, terribly immutable.

Trunk wavers and twists.

And on an agate edge the head turns wildly with its blurred wings of ears, emitting its shrill blue and bright bulbray.

God

The Dramatist sat working. He saw his hero young, handsome, and gifted with valuable gifts. He saw him married, weighed down by life (it was a Tragedy, 'bien entendu'). He saw him finally overcome. He grew sad when he thought of his hero, sometimes even wept. Often he said to himself: 'There, but for the grace of God, goes...'

Then the play was staged and was an instant success. Touring companies were sent out, translations made. The play was performed in every capital in Europe. But the Dramatist had forgotten the old play, for he was working on another.

And every night while the Dramatist slept, ate, entertained, loved: at eight o'clock precisely a certain theatre in London would be filled with beautiful women in beautiful wraps, virile men in evening dress, shop girls and clerks in the gallery. At 8.10 his hero would walk on the stage, take off his 'gibus' with verve and develop his part. The heroine would fling herself into his arms, threaten suicide; in short be adorable. The whole long play would be gone through, word for word as it had been written, with exactly the right curve of wrist for holding a cigarette. To the Dramatist, when he thought about it, these were people he had met vaguely at dinner.

On the continent at varying times the same scene was enacted. The same sort of theatre was filled with the same sort of people who were shown the play exactly as it had been written, word for word.

Another replica of the hero; an identical heroine: angry, sobbing, despairing. The same emotions evoked all over the world.

And every evening, while the author of their being slept, ate, loved or entertained; somewhere a thousand miles away a beautiful, straight and immaculate hero would suddenly break off his own sleeping, eating, entertaining or loving to knock at a door, walk on to a stage, throw his 'gibus' on to a divan, and pull up his trousers a little at the knee before he knelt to make his grand declaration of passion. Every evening, a hundred similar heroes and heroines all over the world.

It was like an action that, once done, goes careering through space forever and forever.

But the Dramatist was working on a new play. He had forgotten what his old play was about. He even repeated one of the scenes, with a difference.

Monkeys

1.

In the large Ape house, they saw 'Jacky', the young gorilla. She sat on a chair and he climbed into her lap, and put one long arm round her neck and the other across her breast.

He turned his face to the keeper with a timid expression as though to say — 'You see, I am behaving myself.'

She was very pleased with him. He was affectionate, yet well-bred and undemonstrative, and the hairy arm tickled her face pleasantly.

She sat very still as with a lover.

He reminded me of myself — once, I sat so — musing vaguely — hour by hour.

2.

Jacky's cage was underground, but from the windows he could see a path with people walking. He sat on the ledge watching the white skirts flicker by his window.

Dreaming with his chin on his hands.

3. *Silvery Gibbon*

She shrank back on her perch into the darkest corner of the cage and gazed at us mournfully and intently through the silver hair that fell wildly over her face. Nor did her gaze waver while we stared with hostility at her, from a distance safe beyond the dart of an angry and skinny paw.

In that enduring gaze of starved motherhood, I saw Ophelia.

Always the same intent gaze and it was clear that the time was long since passed when she had ceaselessly padded the cell waiting for the wicket to open.

They did not know why she had gone mad, but I thought of my mother.

God Bless the Bottle

A remote and hitherto untouched aspect of man is his relation to the bottle as vehicle. The philosopher, engaged in an instinctive process of denigrating his fellows, begins to see man as a more than laborious ant appurtenance of an indubitable egg; occasion for sudden alarms and heroisms. Story has it that ringed by fire instinctive processes madden him, make him swallow his burden, knowing that still it will persist in the heart of the race. The unexpected oblation fills him with strange intoxication. Whether the brain grew spongier or sudden contractions exuded new and never before envisaged possibilities is the problem set before us.

Nevertheless there would seem to be no occasion of life without its bottle. In at the front door, out at the back, life itself could not be more simple. These bottles are of as many species as they who minister; relieving them of the burden of a self-sufficient existence. From the expansible djinn of a carboy to the dwarf (atom moulded to bottle shape for the dolls' service) they range with an equal-relative density, the thousandfold refined essences of science attain to an homeopathic dose. To all these man responds. This test of man as G.C.M. should once and for all prove his adaptability placing him anywhere in an infinite descending and ascending series. Des Esseintes has never been that exotic the 90's found him, for all men are his peers.

As a detonator for the dramatic that jigger embedded by a benign provi-
dence so close under the skin of strong and weak the bottle is of course with-
out parallel. The little heart begins pumping, the moderately large blood
streams race, the little brain flops all over the place; a corner begins to chatter
like the whirring of a dynamo. One is flung off at a tangent plotted equidistant
to time and space with geometrically increasing velocity. This you will admit
is considerably more to the point than all the bombs improvised out of empty
bottle, powder and rusty nails, and the mode of ingestion is by so much the
more dignified. The analogy is that of a water mattress. What was empty
swells, assumes the vertical, rigidity, even gives itself airs; is no longer the
creature of circumstance. It has become rock-like in comparison. Why intro-
duce a brain which now assumes merely its real and eternal function of
emanation. That is so much to the good.

Divagations in the manner of the Purple Pileus need not detain us, but
half a dozen bottles passed out of the back door with a hollow gurgle of the
belly is more dispiriting than any carcase — for here was that indubitable
afflatus which makes man so rare a creature, just as the completeness of its
lack makes man more vegetable than phanerogams, more salt than a mineral.

And there are certain human essences Science would do well to bottle.
Musk is not so far removed as certain flower essences.

I have met people whose essences attain vast proportions in rooms,
themselves as tight as any spider in the centre web deployed around them.

Chanson on Petit Hypertrophique

J'entends mon coeur qui bat
C'est nanan qui m'appelle.
          — Laforgue

Limpid efflorescence of light gradually pervaded me. Nerve endings tingled
and life buzzed continually like bees at a hive. Very remote, systole and
diastole began quietly. Very remote and limpid, and drew nearer until it
burnt and quivered in jabs of red and green and chocolate.

The rhythmic beat grew systematic and while before I had feared lest it
should again fade vaguely into its origins, now my fear dropped and I could
freely eat of the continuous and singing buzz of life, rocking me endlessly
through the electric blue-green night.

And the buds of my joints developed each its separate entity, swarmed
off from the parent so that I throbbed tiringly with my eccentric regions of
systole and diastole. The life in each joint grew more potent. My existence
was less individual. I was unable to seize knowledge of my identity. My
origins, clear and obvious to me before, lost their sharpness. I could not
think or be aware of myself. Too much stress of life confused and amazed

me. What was my mother now? Willingly I would have laid hold on her entrails to tear, had she wanted to thwart me, but she was now no longer concerned to prevent me. Quietly and, to me, a little simply, she allowed herself to be the tool of my life. Then I would hug myself with joy in the hot close corner, as one assured of certain deliverance and who knows there is the world for him.

Quiet and the green and red and chocolate gave place to orange and my head was streaked with fine nets of palpitating crimson and a nimbus of fire rose from it quivering endlessly. And like cotton-wool it remained ever between myself and the strained and despairing heart of my mother.

I was conscious of ether, an oil bubble on its large surface — of nebulæ tenuous as my own life — at times thinner and more tenuous even, so that I shuddered before incommunicable darkness. Again I withdrew into my hot wet corner.

And Night came again and with more intensity. I shuddered with foreboding feeling the parent life ebb, and yearningly and undeniably I clutched fast to the life-giving entrails.

So for a long time.

My mother could not tell what to do. She wanted me, but hated the thought of being tied. It was a struggle between our separate desires for life, but hers was a losing game, for she only half wanted to win. And the great cold gave place to great heat and that again to great cold and the intricate scarlet threads leapt madly through me. In anguish I could have said, 'Let me go,' but again she would not and through endless periods of time held me fast adding clay to clay with a sure yet wavering thumb.

Primeval darkness enwrapped me and the smells of steaming savannahs, the green pond and the tiger's musk.

I felt nails and teeth and to tear with them.

Gradually I knew less of my mother. My prescience wavered and fled, leaving only the memory that it had been, and like a sultry hermit I wrapped my cloaks more tightly about me, adding cloak to cloak to shut out the irrelevant world of my mother and her thoughts.

At certain periods the cloaks would become transparent and again there would be remote prickly nebulæ, sticking fine needles through me. Quickly I buried myself within my cloaks and again darkness and the urgent buzz of life, working obscurely.

And quietly and more quietly life seized me. I was aware of light, of density and of milk.

Then grey-green electric darkness spluttered with blue sparks between pole and pole.

Mr Segando in the Fifth Cataclysm

In 1940 Segando was gathered to his fathers and canonised. In 1950 came the fifth cataclysm, in very little distinguished from the fourth save that it celebrated its inception by the foundation of a Segando research committee. Starting with such works as 'When the sleeper wakes' and 'A story of the future' with divagations to 'The crystal egg', they laid down roughly the lines to be avoided. No centralisation, all modes of progression other than by foot (thirty categories) to be strictly penal, no artificiality of milieu but artificialities of demeanour.

Men with wide shoulders and wasp waists were encouraged. Women were preferred with large waists, larger posteriors and very small shoulders. The ideal female torso was an isosceles triangle — man's the inverted.

The strictest homologies with contemporary colloquialisms had to be observed, and the eternal triangle was, if anything, more ubiquitous than to-day, save only in practice; for by this time both men and women were rather bored with each other. Intercourse was a matter of passing the time of day; the sentimental pressure of a hand and so on.

Their research into Mr Segando carried them still further. These cataclysms dated from the first in 1941 — by some called the people's revolution — the others occurring at odd intervals. In the third, a crowd of fanatics flooded the S.R.C. and proceeded to invent Eadhamite, moving stairways, speaking cinematographs. Life was speeded up to incredible intensity and London grew so rapidly and complicatedly that thousands of people had never been outside their parish in forty years. Fortunately the fourth cataclysm, which some traced directly to irritation caused by the S.R.C., put a stop to that. They went back in a direct line to Bacon, Morris, More. They canonised Mr Hudson, and everywhere tiny communities on the lines laid down in 'The Crystal Age', grew up. Long buildings, such as were found by Russell Wallace on the Rio Negro and Orinooko, 125 feet by 25 feet, became the communal dwelling places, divided into a kind of horse box, one for each individual; while the centre was occupied by the head man. These houses were like nothing so much as a glorified Liberty's, with each cubicle the home of a craft.

To restrict the birth rate (their only really serious problem) it was decided that each child must be answered for by the death of one parent. The death of both, though not obligatory, was yet approved as a noble gesture.

Difficulties arose as may be imagined, and in the first years the number of orphans was prodigious. Certain romantic spirits produced children purely from bravado and anxiety to make a fine end. These, in course of time, were canonised. Religion was a definite Positivism, and the excessive number of saints involved the year in 1,001 days. By this time, as may be imagined, Astronomical science had reached a very high pitch.

The S.R.C. of the fourth cataclysm had a very good time. They spent a lot of money in testing appliances. They experimented on themselves in the matter of speed, of ingested vegetables, of concentrated foods, converting themselves for the purpose into the most exquisite 'Des Esseintes'.

64

At this time Mr Porjes invented a machine having male and female elements exquisitely balanced, and *en rapport* with the mathematical equation he had evolved of Mr Segando's remains. Mr Segando was called back to take his place on a beloved earth. With the hideous callousness of inventors Mr Porjes promptly died, carrying with him his secret, having previously put Mr Segando down in the Lympne he loved so well. You see him rather diffident in a very simple world. Everybody was on the land, i.e. on six square feet of back garden, which, under intensive culture gave all that was wanted. There were no factories, but certain public works were compulsory. Food was generally uncooked, but latitude was allowed. Clothes were somewhat complicated variations on the equilateral inverted trunk triangle for men, and the isosceles generally for women; though indeed the equilateral was also a type. A triangle which threatened two acute angles was strangled at birth. Perhaps with too great a fervour had they flung themselves into a back to Nature stunt, for habits which interfered with the development of the individual were encouraged. Originality in small things was permitted, but only as a safety valve for a possible 'village Hampden'. Initiative was punished first by a fine, and then by a long period of banishment. It was found that solitude so destroyed the virus of public-feeling and emulation that thereafter the outlaw became the most model and reactionary of citizens.

The type grew every day more stable, but unaccountably (generally in spring) large masses would willingly engage in the laying of roads, digging of canals, afforestation, &c.

These storm centres were found to correspond to leading articles in the *Times*, and the population was therefore gently jockeyed into useful works by a timely article or so.

Much stress was put on the value of ideals in education. Education in those days was a continual university extension lecture. Each lecturer was bound by his seat to finish every lecture with the words, 'As we hope for a better world.' This phrase had become the password of the Britisher — cheerio was forgotten in the land — but heads were bowed in silent meditation when the orchestras of that time played the bars, 'As we hope for a better land', to a tune not unlike 'At the end of a perfect day'. People lived in calm reflective amity with suitable reflections for each daily event: —

To thine own self be true. —

It's a long road that has no turning. —

A thought in time saves nine.

The cataclysms had destroyed most calculating machines. The S.R.C. thought it was absurd to use a unit which had only an arbitrary existence for the measurement of real things. They said that such a conclusion was fit only for mathematicians and scientists — for all of whom they had only the strongest contempt. Instruments, therefore, and measurements of whatever kind were now obsolete and life was so much the more exciting.

All Mr Segando's attempts to comprehend the state of things met only with failure. He could find no particular reason for the simplicity of living, or why so many idealistic waves had swept the country. In 1925 it had become prohibitionist; in 1926, on the ground that smoking encouraged drinking and vice versa, smoking was stopped. M. Galopin's 'L'Alcoöl, Le Tabac et la Folie' was resuscitated. The civil war ensuing was more idealistic and much more bitter than any war of liberation. From the abolition of these things it was a short step to the destruction of elaborate furniture, in *auto-da-fe*'s outrivalling Savonarola's. Finally, the country settled down to one room per person. A child became a person at twelve. Before then it belonged to the State. A strong movement to abolish clothes, heat and machinery at one operation failed because of its too ambitious nature. Either would most certainly have succeeded, but so sweeping a measure only ended by terrifying even its most vehement adherents, and for a breathless moment giving the smoker and drinker a hope of better things. Lest the reader imagine however that this was due to American influences, I must point out that the whole population of that unhappy continent had at one operation emigrated to England, in despair of ever gaining culture.

By rising with the sun and sleeping at dusk much labour was saved.

Work was somewhat laborious because an eminent mathematician had calculated that through all its processes, plus the digging of coal, it took longer to create a machine than to do the work with primitive implements.

Life was a garden suburb. Each had a rose bush, a vine attached to his rather unpleasantly large cubicle (since small rooms led to precocity, and throwing the spirit back upon itself produced what was commonly known as art).

Mr Segando seemed to himself to be drifting through a grey green world where dim boneless shadows continually hit up against him; shadows engaged in activities he could not fathom. The conventionalization of sexual relations staggered him; he would not have believed that the most fundamental of the instincts could be so set at naught until he remembered how taboos of all kinds had made this a very usual procedure with savages. Anguish of mind made him gesticulate in his stride; he became an object of curiosity and terror.

Reverence for the aged was still an important feature of this people. Their strong impulse towards punctilio made it very difficult for them to avoid reverence.

In those days people were neither happy nor unhappy. They did not therefore exercise themselves over a future life, duty to one's neighbour, &c. There was very little in which a man might be indebted to you or interfere with you. He couldn't want your goods; two beds and two chairs would have made him ridiculous, they would have tried him for attempting to revive the absurd practices of cohabitation. You had no wife and there was no adultery. The whole business was so simple that even were you passionately centred in another being, when she transferred her affections it was without the engagement rings that so complicate this life of ours; the commitments in the matter of house taking and furniture buying. Out of all this fooling something was growing. Certain internal features were hardening;

soon there would be a skeleton. The important thing was to find a means of utilizing the long periods of leisure. It was hardly enough to lie about all day meditating on how good the sun was; how cleverly green had been invented to rest the eyes. You were very punctilious, and every day you thought of a new refinement of manner.

When I left they were contemplating a lamb that had strayed in from the country. They were asking each other what might be dispensed with to make themselves equally engaging. Mr Segando had almost disappeared.

HYMNS (1920)

Hymn to Love

Ave Maria, Stella Maris
Ah Paris
Yet even in London,
Brantôme, Whitman,
Vatsyayana.

Even so
can it be merely
a matter of
(quoting De Gourmont)
mucous surfaces?

O impossible virginity
of ductless glands!
The agony!

Yet maybe they too are happy.

For I have heard
there *is* an odour of sanctity
and it is real —
like musty clothes —
but the odour of venery,
goats and laurels —
is flung
six feet through a room,
and remaining,
fires lovers to perpetuate it.

Restraints!
coyness — blushes,
trembling knees,
fluttering eyelids,
working throttle-
mad hands —
how terrible your impotence!
how pitiful!

A bull in a slaughter-house,
his knees in curdled blood —
weeps.

First loves.
Tragedies of incompetence —
misunderstandings —
tragedies of haste and fear.

Second loves.
Tragedies of satiety;
clever and wanton aimlessness.

Third loves.
Bah!

When the moon's full
yellow, sordid, wrinkled —
we rise to the surface of our
velleities — Ascidians —
to play at passion
yellow and wrinkled.

Ave Maria Stella Maris.
White Ewe of the Canting Crew

Hymn to Heat

Viscous atom crawls and creeps from atom
and like a snake uncoiling
they hump themselves in ridges,
O eternally insatiate.
O yearning ones.

Under her caressing fingers,
Desire wells up in you.
You swell...strive nearer,
O Proud Erection!
She is a magnet
and Ark of life.

Viscous atom crawls and creeps from atom
and like a snake uncoiling,
slow — then fast and faster
they flow out to meet you

Insatiable whore!
You suck them into your eternal
and alchemical vagina —
absorb and renew them.
Insatiable whore!
Incestuous.
Foul mother, fond mother —
Mother.

Mother
Transcend us   renew us
and atom from atom will creep —
viscous —
and like a snake uncoiling,
slow — then fast and faster
desire well up in us.

So erecting ourselves,
in proud incest
fructify you.
Swirl madly
to your immortal
profound and prolific
vagina.

Call us — O mother.

Hymn to Cold

Sneer on my beloved's lips!

Ultimate!
Naught can evade thee.
Thou imprisonest gases
into strong waters.
Waters to metals.
They can burst earth!
    What then?

    Sneer on my beloved's lips!

The mad flight of atoms
concentres — breathless:
hesitates...
huddles in fear...

   Sneer on my beloved's lips

Thy weapons snow and sleet.
Snow is a white down subtler than seas
burying dead men's secrets.
Your hair spread out about them,
tears each skin off.
Your sleet-spears pierce the heart.

   Sneer on my beloved's lips.

Thy frosts rend mountains,
thy spears rend hearts —
thy hair maidenly
veils the rubbish.

   Sneer on my beloved's lips.

O ultimate poles!
we must march out to thy fires.
In thy wastes
the north lights dance like sphygmograms
in coats of many colours.
   O sneer on my beloved's lips

O terrifying poles!
O howling wastes!
Flame that can flicker and be cold
dances in coloured coats.
O cold — cold cold — maddening cold.
Blood
thou dost freeze in a moment to
Ice.
We stand — Lot's wives —
the snow piles a mound over us —
sleet shoots at the Aunt Sallys.

O Poles!
O cold — fiercer than fierce heat.
O bleak unimaginable wastes.
The snow whirls forever —

it whirls forever
and falls softly.
It raises our mounds
without sound.

O moon!
home of the north wind
home of snow and sleet.
They slide down thy beams softly whirling.
Thy ghastly leer upon our barrows
dements the rescue party.
Hark! they're baying.

Dead — we will climb your beams,
kill you...

Cold!
thou canst turn gases to waters,
waters to metals...
Yah — who showed it you?
Alas we did not teach thee to congeal blood
or bind brains in swift ice.

The north-lights flicker furious in swift sphygmograms,
the snow whirls gently
our brains congeal
each limb grows ice —
the barrow rises, rises.

O moon, O cold, O howling brain-binding waste
thou art a sneer on my beloved's lips.

Hymn to Death 1914 And On

'Danse-Macabre' Death.
'Dried-guts' death.

They clatter, girn, mow —
femur rattles skull
epiphyses shriek, grate —
Brain   a shrunk pea
quintessential lusts —
rattles
rattles   rattles
rattles.
O the 'bones', the wonderful bones.
[God's the darkey]

Toes out, click heels, March!
Evert backbone March!
Breast bone out March!
Shoulder blades well drawn back —
Thumbs to trouser seams —
hold chins firm March
March   March
March!

Danse-Macabre Death.
Dried guts death.

Hi there
take your toes out o' me ribs.

They clatter, girn, mow —
pea brains rattle,
rattle   rattle
rattle.

                    *

Her bouquet at this ball
the sweet skull of her lover.

Hymn to Himself
Atlas 20th Century

Bilge of sneers, insults, kindnesses,
and obligations;
by me and to me,
swinks in the hulk
like a ball of plaster of paris
in a rat.

I can't keep going long with that inside me.

Hymn of Hymns

God damn Cosmoses —
Eternities, infinities
and all that galley.

God damn
white mushroomy flaccid
and smelling of old clothes
Man!
whether Homeric
or after
Dostoievsky.
Born between excrements
in death returning:
Futile cunning man —
[By cunning overcoming the life-inertia.]
Attacking the stars
from eyes five feet above ground.

God damn
woman
mushroomy flaccid
and smelling of old clothes woman.
Her heirs and assigns
for ever.

God damn
the prurulent pestilent wind,
and the pullulating sea.
The eternal infinite, cosmical, blue,

deep, unfathomed, boundless, free,
racing, wild, mysterious sea —
its argus-eyed, winged and lanthorned dwellers.
And you   Walt.

God damn the swift fiery wind
the close comfortable clouds.

God damn
and eternally destroy
the twilight labour of water works,
where in the pumping room
sure pistons work —
[satyriast's beatitude.]

God damn
the incredible tragedies of their geometric ponds
fringed by poplars.

God damn streets
whose dust sends up syph and flu
diarrhœa and smallpox,
whose mean houses hold mean lives,
wallpaper, flypaper
paperfaced brats.

God be with you, Reader

Gas Fire

The sparse blue flame
pulses and pours
through salamander asbestos,
annulated like arteries —
Like a seraph's blood
   [when he sees the sylph]
rushes fast and faster
and whelms in white fire.

Or — like an earthworm
pulsing a thin lymph.

Or like a message
through nerves hid in vertebræ.

The sparse blue flame purrs,
hastens — pauses again —
purrs loudly, gently . . . hissing
forced from what outer spheres;
god   the gasometer.

Three Poems

In Spring women stand like
daffodils. Sometimes they
tremble and touch the bodies
of their lovers.

*

You're like those horrible
castrated lilies. Stamens cut
lest rutting soil your bellies.

*

Night and the ghost forms
rise from sewer manholes like
treasured memories.

I'd have loved you as you
deserved had we been frogs

Where did I hear of two smooth frogs
clasped among rushes
in love and death:
rigid and with spread fingers.

And we   men
all brain, all heart, hot blood;
turn lightly, then
'Ah, weren't we once friends?'

The Dancer Dancing

My blond idol's on fire.

And then to have her so
that with such heat
she'd whelm me out of life.
There would be neither flame nor smoke,
but in a flash
white ash   about her navel
I   Phoenix through her fires.

The Scourged

Under the whips of men
the skin shreds off.
I bleed from every pore.

Men do not see me
staggering between their houses
shivering and making a slobbering noise
like a child.

Pregnant

The ripe fruit waits to drop
till some quick fear
loosen it.

Seed, fruit
flower long shed, forgotten.
Root
feeds on rotten
slimes of fear.
Yet that must tear
what held it there.

Chryselephantine

Comet-dust
Your eyes are magnificent
Odilon Redon's;
bovine
and oppressive.
Lips   granite
Nose   forged steel
Chin   iron
set in their bronze sockets
on a chrysoprase skin.
White jade neck
and all
framed in your blue black eyebrows and
thunder of hair.

And fire thrills, floods —
wavers through you,
in subtle osmoses;
and though you did not know me yesterday
yet you have yielded in a flash
and I
why I am english, lady
and bow to you.

Inventory of Abortive Poems

These are the poems in my head.
August last year in Glastonbury
and the intensity of our life there.
This to be complete
in under one hundred and fifty lines.

The poem of the 'Mass of Shadows'
to form a considerable work
and win renown among poets.
    A long poem for those places I shall never see.
    An acrostic on the name of one I loved
and the letters of whose name
are as many as the lines of a sonnet.
    Also a poem to the same
full of scorn yet tender.
    A sonnet in the manner of Verlaine.
    A poem in the manner of Jammes.

81

Lamps

Piccadilly Cyclops
bowed — head on hands —
watches men.
Fixed violent eye
hurls light.

Charging rams hide men.

From a Biography

I

He was a spider inside a tumbler,
a miserable gannet caught by wire.
Light flooded the galleries
and men glowed transparent against
the high windows.
    Outside his window women played tennis.
In a warder's house women took tea.
Always the trains slipped slyly into Clapham Junction,
and aeroplanes crawled across his window.
He woke in sunshine, fell asleep in sunshine.
The smell of his armpits suffused him with longing.
He read Job and the Song of Solomon.
'Peau de Chagrin' and 'Venus and Adonis'.
He had forgotten moon and stars
And remembered her only to hate her.
Life had ebbed from him, his past was forgotten.
It was a story read in a book.

II

There was an afternoon of speechless anguish.
He made noises like a hurt dog.
Wanted to cry but could not;
He could not contain himself: strode the cell feverishly.
His heart was bursting and his throat too big for it.
Looked out of the window trying to sob.
Saw mock him the tall towers of the Lots Road Station.
And Eveline who lived under them,

would be going to the Café.
The sky darkened: a strong wind blew:
fanned the smouldering dung heap.
It burst into flame, flared and flapped proudly:
he thought of himself, and his bitterness faded.

Under the Trees

I sit,
a stone.
Empty, black, diffuse;
one with this spongy mould
and quiet.
I sit,
bleak and friable,
and a wind whistles itself quietly
into distance.
And the trees clink the gold,
which is so thin, so cold, so immeasurably remote.
All is become metallic —
Salt   bitter   very still.

   Inert
I sit. And all the débris of ten thousand years
snows me under.
Godlike,
inert,
bleak and friable,
porous like black earth,
I sit —
where quietly
pitters the ruin of ten thousand years.

Deserted Wife

Anguish tugs hearts through tugging entrails.
Projects wide arms and writhing fingers,
To clasp, compress, make palpable wide air —
to stuff that aching hollow.

    (Affection was a mutual plug: he's gone, and
      leaves her empty; the wound takes cold.)

    Then fevered nights...
Frayed hair blurring white blankets.
She feels as dead as furniture
lost in vast rooms:
No whispered name makes the shadows leap.

    No more in timid counterpoint
she answers the male chord,
No more mutes its clangour
or timidly feigns power.
That mountain sheltered delicious valleys.

    Now — thrust out to the spent places —
harried by rain, by stinging sand,
made to make up her mind
she gives up, stretching a skinny neck after him.

Dancer

This is Niobe
whirling in anguish
over her dead ones!
gathering the poor strayed limbs.

Whirling she sucks them into her
they fade through and into her;
Her swiftness whirls the air into one large round sob.

Now a bitter ellipse — wickedly whirling:
so tight — so crushed by air:
so shaped by the thumb of air
and levered on humming heels;
her pointed head
drills the skiey vault:
makes heaven's floor tremble!

Wax Dummy in Shop Window

Avalanche pickled in splintered quartzes — Andean,
among light — cones that stalked
muttering above house-tops like gods
or a shrill pendulum.

Light slipped in the wash of scuttling taxis
Loud water rolled.
Aspidistras!
Squalls waken in the fan-whirr.
Evening — flamingoes.

Rain — loud bee swarm
Thunder — his hair tingled.

Stalagmitic — fought to break brain ice
burst spar-eyes
for women, buttered — smiling weakly

Wide street — a wide river light streaked.
green faces swim out, stare at him,
flatten noses protrude eyes
recede in prisms.

Light cones stand desolate.
God: Pickled in splintered Quartzes.
Blue night — green pavement.

'The Pale Hysterical Ecstasy'

White face puffs out — cobra's hood,
age wrinkles at lip corner —
glands flash open [though ductless]
a black draught for blood stream,
the spate boils on the dams.

Perceptions smash through brain —
a ball in a skittle alley
thrown by a drunk.
Instincts shut, open, shut —
the flute note.

That buddha squat
the alternative
broods nobly;
pointing upward and onward.

Usual throat gulp and heart ache —
the sum of them flees distracted
through an old forest
well known, but forgotten with agony.

If then eye white turn up —
tic play a devil's tattoo
fear lard each limb with sweat-ice
loins distend with pain —
she sighs and is justified.

Wild West Remittance Man

Schlemihl no mother weeps for
doomed for a certain term...

Ryewhisky...a fungus
works into each face-line...
the bondstreet exterior...
tears at his vitals...
gravely the whisker droops
his eyes are cold.

Immaculate meteor!
Inside a thick ichor
outside a thick ether
quenched the bright music.

Body linings peel
from the deep core
in siroccos of Alkali.
england...thy drawing rooms...
sundays...mahogany...
the fire leaps.

Ryewhisky!
shuffle of counters. . .
revolvers, marked cards.
A million tons of locust-sirocco
blasts and grinds.

And the cayuse snorts by
hey-up. . . hey up. . .
shots. . . the loud greeting.

He turns to the counters. . .
rustling paper. . . marked cards;
gravely the whisker droops
his eyes are cold.

OTHER POEMS 1913-1927

Deidre is Dead

Only his kisses corroding
Other things having their will...
That are soon still —

The grey winds start
Fearing what fear?
Phantasmal peer
Lily-white faces —
Without three paces
Breaks the world's heart —

The deeps of her hair
Surge far and wide...
Can darkness stride
That hollow place...
Or all God's grace
Sear a light there?

I never saw her
That was so proud
Nor saw of the crowd
Still hurrying after...
With sere secret laughter
Where her feet were...

Only his kisses corroding
Other things having their will
And they're soon still.

Webster

Murder and rape and sudden quick alarms —
Rustling quick inrush of paid panders with drawn arms:
The guttering flambeaux breathing odorous balms
Thrill the dead-drooping arras. Unashamed
Brute Lilith sways in the lecherous light
And leers in anguish o'er her vanished charms;
Her lust-drawn cheeks and body livid framed —
Shriek upon shriek upon the gathering night
Marks justice, blinded, pinned and maimed.

In the Courtyard

A shell smashes...
The world lifts
upon this wave of nothingness
which throws us up...
Crashing us upon the toothed rocks of the air
till we fall mangled, bleeding, hysterical...

It is as though some verminous rag
were shaken clean, then dropped in the old place —
Life carelessly invests it...

In peace,
a cut finger made my heart bleed more
than all these 'mangled limbs'
these 'fair bodies murdered in their prime',
outraged women, mutilated children.

Not the spattering bullets
make me think of hail
the coolness of rain,
the curves of English downs,
low dark clouds that enfolded me close
but yesterday.

No! it was not yesterday.
Many days have passed...

A screaming shell tears the sky
Bursts...

The rag's clean again

Dead Queens

'There come not now... such gold-giving lords.'

Women of large hips, small breasts,
And high white shoulders,
Red hair plaited
And pale steadfast eyes,
You are the high romance —
Lilith, Iseult and Guinevere;
You were strong lovers,
Not caring to be loved.

Always your lovers fared the perilous quest.
Patiently maybe you waited,
Maybe loved another —
What mattered it?

All passion was in you, all sweetness.
Your lovers in the far-off courts of kings,
Feasted... tarrying with many women.

Patiently you waited,
Maybe loved another —
What mattered it?

Dead queens, dead queens,
Your lovers left you
When cheeks grew pale, lips faded —
Yet you'd not tie them to you
With their pity.
Dead queens!
In that twilight
Where you lived when love had left you,
Often the rumour came
Of Tristrem and of Lancelot
Riding afar...
Yet that was nought to you...
Time flies, love dies and must die,
Why weep then?
In your kings' beds
You'll not remember
The sweet or bitter of love.

Lilith laughs at the old Adam,
Caught serpent-wise by the swart eastern woman
God gave him to his sorrow!
Her sorrows are his sorrow,
Her thoughts his thoughts;
For she has bound him to her
With the strong toils of his pity —
His heart would burst to break them.

Because Some Lover

Because some lover in some darkened place
Leaned brooding towards the face of his dear,
Till after a long silence her white face
Would droop towards him, and lip to lip
Half touching, fearful lest their senses slip
Bonds and whelm them in a clear
White flood of passion, they remain
Lips touching, yet apart; fierce strain
On interlocking fingers —

Some poet wrote it down,
And that old story lingers,
Your only crown,
Lancelot, Abelard, Paolo and Pelléas:
To too many women have you brought undoing.

Too many women have been read
The stories of your fates,
And always when was said:
'. . . leaned brooding towards the face of his dear,
Till after a long silence her white face
Would droop towards him, and lip to lip
Half touching. . . fearful lest their senses slip
Bonds and whelm them in a clear
White flood of passion they remain
Lips touching, yet apart. . . fierce strain
On interlocking fingers. . .'
Then leaning towards each other
On limb and separate feature the glance strays and lingers,
And, drooping each to other,
Half kiss, half droop apart
Under intolerable strain.

Too many lovers have you brought undoing:
Sick heart
And great pain.
You, Lancelot and Guinevere,
Paolo and Francesca;
You, Abelard and Heloise,
Pelléas and girl Mélisande,
And that first lover in some darkened place
Drooping to a white face.

In a Garden

There was a paved alley there,
Apple trees and a lush lawn —
And over the gray wall where the plums were
Stood the red brick of the chapel.
While over the long white wall
Where the green apples grew
And the rusted pears
Hung the gray tower of the church;
So high, you couldn't see the top
From that narrow garden.

In that narrow garden, on that lush lawn,
We found a ball left from some croquet game.
It had a blue stripe girdling it,
And, 'Ah,' I thought,
'It is your soul about me,
And we are flung
Between our separate desires.'

In that narrow garden
On the lush lawn,
We flung this ball to each other.
My eyes were only for your legs, your arms.
Under that hot sun,
The hard ball hurt my hands,
Made them hot and prickly,
And I'd have stopped
But feared losing you —
While you too stayed on playing —
— 'Ah, if I'd but known —
Because you would not have me go.'

95

We played so long,
I'd ceased to think —
All thought, each sense,
Rapt in the shimmering circumference;
The blue stripe girdling it
Shone in the sky.

Then I seemed looking down
From some far field,
With this ball one of worlds
Scorned
And cast from each to other,
Blue water girdling them —

By and by the tea-bell rang.

Spring Suicide

Is it because they cannot bear the strain
of green sap mounting body and brain
that suddenly the worn heart snaps
that late beat safe in town traps,
or where the mouldering edge of the rise
was the whole world to their mad eyes?
But yet the noisy street was cold
and cold the wild hillside.

All the hot summer they wander lost.
They know not why they weep in desolate places
in green brakes wonder at white faces,
and in far glades fly the white nereids.
Soft eyes of deer then fairer are to them than any maid's
and on the wide hillside and on the heath
they lie beneath the rutting bear
and eyes, stars, eyes, stars threaten them.

Autumn for them is rotting leaves
good smells, and quiet while night weaves
cold dismal mists that twist
into the ash-poles — sad tryst
moon keeps with the white lake.
And if the trees shake
they do not fear them, lying there
with the wind whispering in their hair.

They do not fear the stars
or weep under the moon
though their heads go bound in iron bars
and an old tune
sings in each bleak brain.
Silently they merge into shadows under the trees
head hanging on bent knees.

Still, there's a peace they get
when snow is on the ground
and the thudding heart beats cease
and blood flows cool again its usual round,
and once again they enter the old life,
friends, children, wife
nor ever fear the white faces they see never —
and knowing yet of feet that go
soundless on the snow,
do not tremble, though fierce eyes
watch their sighs,
fear nothing, for the snow folds them
in a white shroud, body and soul.

The spring comes and sap wings
into body, into brain.
They do not know why such great pain
should take mortals with strong stings
and jerk poor limbs to each queer whim.
When the sun comes they follow him
over hill, over plain
till the moon drag them on again.
Wandering largely, here, there,
dreaming of winds, green eyes, red hair —
till suddenly the moon is full
the sap leaps — one swift pull
loosens the carking body
that could not tranquil hold the strain
of running sap in body and brain.

Now they're dead.
Moonbeams chill each warm close bed
but cannot move the anguished dust
call how she may, Must, must, must!
And then no more to track the swallow
or see the weak winds bend to and fro
the blue ash branches pencilled thin
on skies the night birds wander in —

or follow the sun or follow the moon
to an old tune
or kiss deers' noses...

The Fair

Down the street we heard
organs blare the latest rag
and could not wait
but ran
between quiet houses
and tall comfortable trees
till, sudden lights blinded us.

... And we are in some province of the blest
where the crowd absorbs the burden of myself
and leaves me quiet —
We wander in some province of the blest
where sudden flares show curious blooms,
strange faces with quick eyes and no bodies...
These they left in nether darknesses —

Fluttering round the flares
I try for a cokernut...

The gypsy girl eyes me and her scorn
crushes my old identity upon me,
then while I take the balls
I am in the dim Basrah bazaar
where frail incense weaves frail dreams
and dropping slow from dreaming fingers
the amber beads fall clicking from hand to hand
odorous
and hard and round...

But the ball is flung...
and the wild girl
daughter of moon and heath
and black and magic sires
sourly throws my prize.

And I'm happy...
am suddenly a mighty hunter.
I chase the wild boar in the eye of the dawn
in the evening I track the deer to his water-hole.
Great snakes with jewelled eyes will glower at me
Great birds will flutter in tense anguish,
and I've tickled her neck
with the cokernut beard
and she shrieks.

But the shooting gallery does not draw me
not the Aunt Sallys...

That's a queer thing
when the cunning rogue
hands you the metal discs;
bids you cover the red one wholly —
till you get lost in impenetrable mysteries
enacted in some province of the blest —
or when he bids you overthrow the cone
with swinging pendulum.

And then we got into the roundabout
and swept down on the pallid fungus of the crowd
Then up into the stars
and down and up in some celestial boat
beyond the nethermost sphere.
While ever
a new rag
set fire into our shoulders and our hips.

Pale faces gleamed about us
and all around the quiet night.
In a sudden stillness
a horse cropped the grass
and we saw the stars.
Till suddenly
the organ pipes would blare out a new rag
and thrill our shoulders and our hips
and we'd dance ragtime on the sward.
Around
the fungus of white faces
envied us and gibbered...

and they were dead
that crowded at the tight shut gate of life,
and anguished knew not how to tell me that my dear
would sure betray me...

Until the organ pipes would blare out a new rag
and thrill our shoulders and our hips
till we'd dance ragtime on the sward.
And all around
the fungus of white faces
gibbered without the tight shut gates of life.

The Acrobats

When they had finished all their tricks,
blindfolded — leaping, somersaulting, forming pyramids —
They crossed the stage in little jerky rushings,
bodies very pink across the footlights
bottoms prominent and shoulders held well forward,
legs detached and stiff, like those of dolls —
and again leaping, somersaulting; made more pyramids
and caught each other from great heights
and all blindfolded —
How we clapped them.

They took the call calmly,
placid and unsmiling like horrible pink dolls.

Suddenly I saw their bellies breathing fiercely.

Atavisms

At ten he met her.
Together they went into the forest.
She wanted to go there.
Something said she'd have no rest
else. Her brain swooned
at thought of fern-smell, spatter of dew
swept from brambles — a few
far stars, quick noises. He'd show
her landmarks while they mooned
up hill and down hill —
stumbling on clattering stones, nought know
on that pale thread of road
save soft eyes that glowed.

She wanted him.
Something said she'd have no rest
till in the quiet of dew, flower-scent;
imminent trees, swift wind, wet wind;
he'd put his head on her breast.
She'd throb to his pulse
thrill to his mind —
want to be trampled by his whim.

Something inside her said,
'You must get away!
You want him, but it must be the way
of your mothers — long ago.
How long — you can't know.
And your head is blank,
and a white mist
is over your mind
but clears a little when you are kissed,
and jerks your blind arms round him
till you find
your pitiful warm lips clinging to him.

He will not understand your whim,
perhaps be afraid of the dark,
hate the smell of ferns — a stark
graveyard smell. Fear the tall trees
as ghosts,
and the branches' groping hands. He's
afraid of the moor's green eyes; of the hosts
of dead rustling leaves that whisper
and rush quietly, stop for a moment, slowly stir.'

Under you there's heather —
What need to stir?

Her arms are about you,
Her warm moist kisses are still on your lips.
But something rustled in the heather about you,
and the warmth that was here now slips,
and the breast that you loved is departed.

Fond lover! is she flown?

Perhaps modesty struck her like a stone,
stunned ancient desires woke up in her.
She hides in the heather — her rustling betrayed her.
Can't you hear her panting...see eyes gleam...on fire
for kisses? Desire
sets torch to her — she's hiding —
says you must find her.
Wants you to find her,
crush her to you — striding
upon her and over her,
bite ear and shoulder
clutch breast to breast —

What thing rustled into the dark?
You will not find it?
You say you've no delight in stark
things you don't understand?
You will go home, not mind it?
'She knows her own mind, plays her own hand!
Is a Romantic fool!'

Snow Pieces

I.

How mournful the snow is when the moon is cloud hid.
It is grey and lies in the road like a mullet.
And then it grows darker and the light dies inside it,
and I want to sleep but can't make my mind up
to blow out the candle,
or to lift myself — then it gutters.
I wish she were here, and I with her

and there were black trees and a terrace
and our feet making footprints,
and she, warm and living and musky beside me.
And the moon came back then and turned her face ghostly
and her eyes into ice-sherds...

II.

Full moon, fresh snow, very white, throwing light up —
Not white, green under lamps, blue in shadow:
it is like her skin, but that is ruddy,
though both shoot luminous daggers at me —
One cold and harsh and intolerable,
the other warm and musky and intolerable.
O unendurable longing —
to crush from each that essential drop
bringing relief! I cannot.
To drench myself in their breathless cold —
eyes, touch and smell —
Then quiet sleep,
When they put soft arms around me!

To Any Idol

You'd have sat here through far ages —
and weary with dim lore they'd put in you
and full of valuable learning
would have smiled and smiled and smiled...
but still I'd not have noticed you.

Till you grew
a rodent strain of verdigris,
and held me
till I looked at you...

and saw your face...

Nude with Wrist-watch

The watch ticks on her wrist.
Will, must, can't but tick on —
And how she writhe or twist
or furbish; her life's gone.

The watch ticks on her wrist,
where she lies on the bed,
measures each moment, kissing, kissed:
Each moment, by what passion fed.

The watch ticks on her wrist.
Her life is naked — its meaning gone —
Her watch in a last tryst
with Time, Space and Decay, ticks on.

Beatitude

I would be like
that naked Aztec.
Red gold powdered — burning, burning —
Bursting on the awed crowd
like sun through clouds —
In that same instant swallowed
plunged in dark lake.

I would be like that flat Aztec skull
wrought in crystal —
having no suture, no dropping jaw:
but only transparent thoughts.
and behind — what sinister something?

I would be like that temple of the sun
a thousand stages, corridor on corridor —
Eternal twilight —
broad flat flights of stairs
in darkness —
terraces
in light —
and at my altars —
ten thousand scummy jumping hearts.

I would be like that Aztec skull
iridescent
with thin turquoise plating.
Underneath —
decaying bone,
dank orbits
sinister —

Then
would I be like that 'peak in Darien'!

The Shop

In the evening after work
when I go down the little side street in Battersea,
to the tiny shop
with its packets of Lyons' tea with blue labels
in the window —
and with them
a pink tin or two of salmon;
and the black and brown boot laces
hang from the gas bracket
with its two pale globes,
a little bell jangles
and the Japanese wind bells tinkle furiously for a minute
and my feet strike loudly on the boards.

After a while
a little old woman with grey hair
comes out and sells me matches.

On the counter is a glass case
with collar studs and tins of blacking.
Wood bundles are stacked against the counter
and I smell the tarred string binding them.

In the air is paraffin
and the strong acid of pickles.
Pickles! Red, yellow —
onions, walnuts, gherkins!
their acid smell is poignant
vertiginous. . .

Yellow or red —
mustard pickles
or the sickening magenta of red cabbage.

I cannot resist them,
they bite into me,
I too, once lost a love —
and so I take the horrible magenta of the red cabbage
in a piece of newspaper —
and the old lady carefully drains off the vitriol.

And the shop grows sombre
and after a while the little old woman
goes out of the shop
to her bright parlour,
where perhaps she has a parrot.

Such a hollow jangling of the bell when I go out
and the wind bells tinkle, tinkle...

Under the Trees VI

Under you, green pyramid,
what King with gold-glued face is hid?

Or are you a lung of earth?
or tadpole gill that to lung will give birth?

Under wind you will not bend!
but shiver, break – glass will bend!

Through your running sap — nights and days
does He see stars always?

Do you wave your leaves at his whim
like his slave waved fan for him?

Do your roots wind him more tight
than cerements — or lie more light?

Or are they dank, and knows he it vain
to writhe in anguish, utter his pain?

Or through his gold-glued skin in agony
to move his eyes or mouth or tongue, does he try?

Are your whisperings
his, or another thing's?

Green pyramid,
tell me — what is there hid?

Under the Trees VII

Your roots, dank, obscene
tapped her eyeballs for your green.

And after, in the late year
they sucked the bronze from her hair.

Your pith
came from her body, snowy, lithe.

Your rough black bark you grew
out of these things — strange and true.

But she is dead and it's in vain
you mimic her to ease my pain.

The Searchlight

The searchlights over London
are like the fingers of a woman,
wandering over the dead form of a lover.

She had not thought to do that
while he was living,
to better know his loveliness
or if she had —
he'd stopped her with his kisses —
Now in her great grief
her fingers are to her
sight and sound and hearing.

By all the ways of sense
she knows him lost to her,
yet cannot voice her grief.

Only can she raise white hands towards the heavens
and passionate cursings and great grief,
yet no sign comes, no portent:
O if one blistering tear would come from on high
to crumple up and twist the earth
she'd know her nightly passion not so vain
when her first pang
burst the heavens with howling of guns.

An Old Story

I
hated Nature!
from that moment when I found
lilies did not spring around
where my sweetheart's foot touched ground —
nor the gate she touched
change a feature —
nor swirl up in fire
taken with desire —
nor was with bright lit fungi smutched.
While the grass on which we lay
crushed for but one day —
now rises in new joy in wind to play.
But Nature's wise —
and it's all one whether she'll wait —
or heap dirt over your sweetheart's eyes:
and soon it's all one to you
whether days you doted were many or few —
an age ago, or an hour or two.

Solace

Evening
and again I go down the chill lane
where we parted.

It is not changed
though it was here we parted.

An old man
stumping on a stick.
He has a wooden leg
and a sack.

Come with me old man!
be my companion;
women are all the same —
pain and pain.

Come be my companion —
you'll sit by my fire when the tramp's over:
if you mumble your food — I won't strike you:
or if you wail for a hearth and bed:
or if you've rheumy eyes.
You'll have quiet with me:
no talk at my fireside:
and I won't talk or think of my sweetheart's bed.

In the Park

Jumble
Of
Heads.
Nerves
Raging.
O Love
Death
Kisses
Each
Rhymer.

Words

Burning her letters one by one
    till all were done,

I leaned over the fire and saw
    the flaw,

of black words flicker on white ash —
    till in a flash

All crumbled, and a sudden heat
    there beat

Around me. Ah words we thought were frail —

Hymn to Nature

Nature red in tooth and claw!

There are those who call you rapacious maw —
there are those who have seen you on windy heights,
a sylph — skirts round slim thighs: strange lights
on streaming hair and on shoulders — olive, mauve, red,
in other lights dun —
some have seen you stark —

Nature red in tooth and claw!

I have seen you a mountain stretching out one paw —
you played with the earth: your bristling hair
Wellingtonias — and where
your bald tail hung over the world's end
the stars were flies
you leapt for, snuffled over, tried to rend
though they stung agonies.

Nature red in tooth and claw!
who taught
the servant girl
with pennyroyal to abort.

In the beginning
you made NOTHING.
Out of this you made the sun —
the sun spat out the earth —
the earth spat out the moon.
They began to wriggle
like cut appendices —
thus instigated orbits.

This was how life began
Nature red in tooth and claw.

For the earth
you made a coat
all about it — and cerulean blue.
It is an old coat now — and frayed
and when the sun is down
worn patches let through light
from other spheres.
The spots on this coat
hid his sire from him —
he wanted to dance naked —
You turned the spots to seas for him.

Earth swinked long years in steaming seas.
By ceaseless gyration and churning
she made
L I F E .
Life made 'more life',
'more life' made the fish,
the fish made the reptile.
In a stage or two
the reptile made man.
Man made seed
and God the woman to take the seed.
Wherefore then did you make pennyroyal —
and not content, the Ergot.

Invoc.   Nature red in tooth and claw
              we adore thee,
              yet those there be
              call thee rapacious maw.
              'for she taught
              the servant girl
              with pennyroyal to abort.'

111

Thou gavest life and takest it,
thou gavest joy and pain.
Thou gavest love and makest it —
Shall it be all in vain?

The calf in the womb
weighs near a hundredweight —
wonderful are thy ways
from cradle to tomb.
But who taught etc.

And too thou hast given us fire
within and without.
Let us praise thee for manifold blessings.

Speak! Art thou a girl that skips upon the hills?
Art thou Moloch burning ever?
Why madest thou the toucans bills?
And shall man dwell in Eternity never?

Thou gavest us metals and all is well!
yet knowest not thyself what things thou gavest.
Lo every day we teach thee more
fumbling in thy skirts.
Take it not ill from us
that we have raped the ultra-violet ray from thee.
seduced and undone thy electrons,
yoked thy arrows, the lightning.

W E showed thee thy strength —
thou showedest us thy hidden ways —
werewolves spawned from thee
tortured our wombs.
Thou gavest a thousand horrors —
Twas thou who taught etc.

Thou gavest us metals
we thank thee.
Thou gavest us life,
we adore thee.
Thou gavest us love
we will magnify thee!
But this disclose to us —
Thou madest love and it is good,
it is pleasant, it is our joy.
We skip upon the hills;

112

Wherefore then madest thou
among herbs good to us,
the pennyroyal and ergot.

For beer and for tea
we may yet glorify thee,
but this, disclose to us.

Nature red in tooth and claw
we worship thee twixt shame and awe,
Twas thou who taught etc.

So we will laud thy ñame forever and forever. Amen.

Hymn to Virginity

O lily white hands!
O meek eyes
untutored — timidly wise,
O body dropping like a flower!

O rapturous hair!

O violet lids —
and violet under the candid eyes —
O green hollows
of cheek and neck.
O bled-pink of lips
and bled-pink when shames rise.

O flower wilting in morning!
we adore thee!
O skinny neck
enslaving at merest beck.

O mystic rites wrapped round you.
Kings have trembled before them.
Strong men been humbled.

O awkward gait!
O timid gaze!
you are beyond praise.

O doe caught staring vaguely
by the pool's edge
flitting shadow, you beckon.

O thing once lost, irrevocably lost —
and glad to be lost,
yet aye lamented: —
if not lost
for me lamented.

The sequel, 'bien entendu',
is dealt with fully in Hymn 2

Hymn to Virginity

The Virgin Sings
>   Lo! we treasured our wine
>   till it went sour.
>   The State stored it for us
>   in the churches' vaults.
>   When we went for it
>   it gave us colic.

Invocation
>   It has gone sour —
>   it has given us colic,
>   spoilt our complexions,
>   eaten away our hearts.
>
>   Therefore love is dead in us.
>   Can we longer believe in
>   the goodness of man
>   and the sons of men?
>
>   Yet stay!
>   maybe one skin
>   ripening more slowly
>   will have marvellous body,
>   be as luminous as new suns,
>   more maddening than wind.

>   *

>   'Vinegar, vinegar, will no one buy vinegar?'

Frogs

We talked of frogs that died in love.
You said, 'Then cold's their heat.'
I wondered, asking why love beat
Quick in them and then shrove
them ever of that heat.
That cold (that heat) given by life
to last through an existence
burst suddenly, an intense
flash, that like a knife
fell, cutting the cord that held it.
That heat was like a liquid gas
that sears what felt it
and bursts, making nothing of what much was.

In green rushes, green they moulder,
smooth, stark,
tight arms round each other, dark
fingers on dark shoulder.

Where is your Tristram now?
Paola's had his day.
Their loves were frail, avow
them play!

A CO's Biography

1.
He being taken she ate the green duck's egg.
Salt waves rolled between them.

2.
Captured.
Before fire in the raw Café. He looked up but
rigid blue columns barred door.
Felt caged already, —

b.
Rigid gas, sour with suspicion.
They search him grimly
— then —

c.
Cell.
Caged in white glaze — Six strides, three strides,
latrine
He was afraid to send for her and part
Yet how he wanted it. . .

Yellow, suffocating gaslight.
Night outside and stars.
She would be waiting.

d.

Morning — horses stamped in mellow yard — dung dried
Children yelled far away and thinly.
All day he wanted to send but dared not
    then evening, night, SLEEP.

e.

Black Maria holds twenty-four in twelve cells
    and between them, a guarded corridor,
Familiar streets again, through a chink Holborn and
    Bow Street and today the sun shines after the
    harsh winter.
The tumbril unravels the road strip by strip.

3.

Khaki cylinders now and he is filled with horror.
Oxford Street — women.
But nobody cares and they even look with hostility
    upon him, avoid him, refuse him cover.

4.
Paddington.

He wavers in a stream of memories in the bitter taste
    of steam.
Weary with longing and fear of the unknown.
The escort sleeps and feverishly he revolves escape.

5.
Newton Abbot.

Thrust into guard room, ten feet cube.
Twelve toucans start to life, flap and crawl, terrify him.
And he shudders and hides himself behind the thought of
    last Tuesday and Piccadilly.
He is button-holed by one who did three years for
    manslaughter, and flashed a chancre cost him a
    shilling.
Acrid smoke of woodbines swirls in dirty yellow
    round the bitter gas mantle.
He marvels at the changes of twenty-four hours.

b.

Folds rugs into bags, heavily and with stiff joints —
    but wears his clothes, lest they be stolen.
Nausea at new intimacies, then sleeps —
turns often in the night, for his aching hips.

c.

Reveille tears tympani —
He wakes into the foulness of twelve bodies sweating
    night long in a sealed room.
And his head swims.
But he had dreamt, was thrilled and relieved...

'Japanese' Whistler; Battersea Bridge in fierce
    cold blue light.
A violent arc lamp and a friend.
One breast was longer and pointed like a fox snout.
He has not eaten for a long time.
The skin sticks to his cheek bones and temples.
Two fierce eyes burn from the yellow parchment.
Innumerable woodbines have made his heart thump and
    flecked his finger nails.
Heaviness grinds all his muscles.
He remembers white sheets and the Chinese Restaurant,
    men come curiously to watch him.
He is the Camp show thing, but the doctor has sent for
    him tomorrow.
She has not written, can she have forgotten?

6.   Effeminate orderlies bathe him slyly.
O opulent warmth.
He sinks into sheets a swooning Ganymede.
His troubles are over, his ticket is sure and he will still see
    spring with her
Stop at quiet pubs —
He smiles like a child, snuggles down — is asleep.

b.   Mad neighing in the night wakes him in fear of terrified
    horses.
The sky blazes with light and points of terror.
An epileptic threshes limbs, neighs shrilly and
Orderlies pad in, stuff pillow under his head.
'He had always been epileptic.' A boy had tripped him.
He had fallen many stairs!
The doctor who passed him got half a crown — but he
    got thirty shillings a week for life.
He could not hide his satisfaction.
He had fits daily; I hated his lizard-like head,
    thick neck, everted nostrils,
    yet his wife clung to him
    and servant girls courted him with cheap cakes.

c.   Because they were mad
They lived in a glazed room
Green with barred windows.
With dusk, eyes leapt from the ceiling
    and one stared straight out from over the door.
The grated peep holes glowed softly and mournfully
    till an eye shuffled darkly behind them.

d.   They tricked him with promise of freedom.
                       He was hungry and wished to believe it.
                       Milk, glutinous and sweet
                              made him blush with blood swirl to head.
                       Then cordial warmth and heaviness inside him.
                       He slept in sweet dreams, warm dreams,
                       In a week they would be together.
                              He waited days. . . then: —
                              'Return him to unit.'

7.   No news.
Guard Room.   He waited.
                       One hour — two hours — three —
                       The light changes — oh — how slowly.
                       A new comer is thrust in, five minutes curiosity
                              and again blankness and waiting.
                       Through individual seconds
                       Then sleep!

b.   Escort
                       And bitter irritation of steam on station platforms
                       And women — stony eyed for him.
                       Spring was not for him, let him die too.
                       He would never again see Fitzroy Street nor the
                              flame of his lover.

8.   Would she come?
                       She clutched his wrist and her fingers worked into
                              his sleeve.
                       Her eyes filled and her breast rose quickly, she
                              clenched her teeth.
                       He trembled to clasp her, but men looked on mocking.
                       Her face was grey and in half an hour they sent her away.
                       It was raining, scent steamed from the grass,
                       She went alone, stunned by suffocating roses,
                              praying:
                       He was far away and for ages.

9.   Blank faces, Charlie Chaplin moustaches —
Court Martial.   Gentlemen of course — barely interested:
                       Six months hard labour in two minutes:
                       Blue sky and a lark shrilling madly.

10.   Bitterness of steam and people in light clothes.
         She did not meet him at Waterloo.
         There was a calm proud woman who did not look at him
            and that made him choke.
         Nothing mattered now, come quickly prison.

11.   He was a spider inside a tumbler, a miserable
Prison   gannet caught by wire.
Wandsworth.   Light flooded the galleries
         And men against the huge windows glowed transparent.
         Outside his window women played tennis —
         In a warder's house, women took tea.
         Always the trains slipped slyly into Clapham Junction,
            and aeroplanes crawled across his window.
         He woke in sunshine, fell asleep in sunshine.
         The smell of his armpits suffused him with longings.
         So he read Job and the Song of Solomon,
         Peau de Chagrin and Venus and Adonis.
         He had forgotten moon and stars and remembered
            her only to hate her.
         Life had ebbed from him, his past was forgotten —
            it was a story read in a book.

b.   He wrote three poems on toilet paper with a smuggled
First Sunday.   pencil.

         If I but opened the door I could walk out.
         I do not want to open the door.
         I am safer in this cell than in the spidery galleries,
            the aery dome,
         I hate the exercise rings — black cinders — that
            circling make me giddy.
         Bed is good though and the coarse sheets — and my
            pied coverlet, hand woven — brick reds,
            yellows and greens:
         I like the sewing and the Bible's interesting:
         And if I opened the door I could walk out.

    To Gretchen, A plaited skein of hemp that hung on the wall.

c.   Margaret beloved! was it the threefold plait of your
            hair that woke the devil raged in Faustus?
         For me, there was 'La fille aux cheveux de lin',
            rather mad.

I stroke you, lay you against my face —
Your hair fine gold, and you hid my face in corn.

I bind each thread over my heart
Sew up my thoughts with them
O glow there on my wall
You will be tied about my heart
When there's nought else to bind it!

Sweet Gretchen, mad Gretchen, most anguished outraged
     Gretchen
I am a wall, my breasts like towers.

d.   After the heavy day —
          rain spatters on cabbage leaves.

I have not missed the sun
     wind I have regretted but not mourned,
Grass trees and pageant of cloud
     content to delight in from my high window
Now life is bitter for these tears do not wet me —
Tears without guile — yet womanly —
     though they crave nothing.
I want to walk out in comfortable sadness
Swathed in dun air —
     my brain's cottonwool for at other times
     the sky's edges cut my brain.

Now the roofs gleam white grey blue
They are quiet like pools
Which tarnish sadly
When twilight shivers over them.

e.   He had a visit. She was thinner than he had thought for.
Her photograph had looked stocky and he had forgotten
     her.
He loved her again but her freedom made him hate her.
She saw green downs moon-rise and stars, sea and wind.
There were other men too.
He teased her gently, his heart was bursting
     but what could he say in twenty minutes.
She said — 'You are not so morbid as you were!'
He would have struck her but wire was between them.
They sent her away.

120

f.   He spoke to the Warder who said food was scarce.
'But there's fruit!'
'No only plums and I don't like them.'
He had not eaten fruit for months.
Three days he saw plums
       pulpy and oozing juices.
His mouth dribbled, he was almost distracted.

g.   He had forgotten the moon and the stars
       till one night they rose outside his window.
From his stool he stared at the four towers
       of the Lots Road generating station
He thought of his mistress moon-mad
       and Orion went away slowly
A warm red light beamed from a window,
       flashed out, they were going to bed.

h.   There were cabbages between the exercise rings
They flapped leaves to the moon, when wind blew:
       like hands in a pit
       or faces thrown up to a Prima Donna.

i.   There was an afternoon of speechless anguish
He made noises like a hurt dog.
Wanted to cry but could not.
He could not contain himself, strode the cell feverishly,
       his throat was bursting and his heart too big for it,
       looked out of the window trying to sob.
Saw the eternal four towers watching him;
And Eveline who lived under them, would be going to
       the Café.
The sky darkened, a strong wind blew
       fanned the smouldering dung heap.
It burst into flame, flapped and flamed proudly.
He thought of himself and his bitterness faded.

12.   Evening — sun flooded his cell.
He had drawn his table under the window,
       his towel a table cloth
       and the bed-boards a back-rest.
He was reading Saint Simon.
The door clicked open, he was told to get ready.

The cell leapt, he tried to steady himself,
Climbed to the window — Ah dear Chelsea:
        lay on the tiles, counted the bricks
        tried to control the quivering lip muscles.

Then following the warder,
        crept through the black antheap
So high — so wide, and the thousand dim arches.

Then the known sergeant:
A bus rumbled, crowds hummed excitedly by them.
Trams clanged, sympathetic women watched him,
They went to a pub and he drank brandy.
Unshaven, without puttees, smiling wanly —
Smoking a gold flake.
There was hay in the air, couples in dark corners,
        all the lost Summer
His head was whirling with smoke like brown paper
        and brandy.
They took him through London.
Would they come with him to her? Yes, then
He found they were taking him to another prison.

13.   He was leaving tomorrow
The place seemed suddenly homely.
He felt mean to be leaving it
        and could not sleep
Stared at the ceiling and thought of her —
        always of her through the slow night.
Sleepless, wondering would she want him —
What would they say to each other?
Then grey dawn and he shivered!

b.   His brain hurt, his eyes watered
Paddington.   he could fix nothing
He felt heroic and stood on the platform
        deafened with khaki.
He regretted his quiet cell.

Theatre

Close held by warm darkness,
wet murmuring darkness,
the crystal ball.

The mellow stage light
transfuses into the skull
and the brain welters in light.

The body forgotten, one with the dark,
one's being nothing —
but it projects a façade
a tall window
which sucks in the light.

And the light breaks in hard splinters
between one's being which is nothing
and the very bright window
which is nothing.

It is all very peaceful
and probably like heaven.
Though far off and thinly
terror runs down a thin wire —
Wells into sound —
Fills the horizon to crush us
with a noise like tearing silk.

Southern Syncopated Singers

Lime's full moon!
The land crabs stalk by on tall fingers.
Birds scream
and steadily march the white ants.

In the full moon of the limes
the pygmies howl to each other
notes piercing sweet and wild.

Their gods stand darkling round them
and the drums make a heavy tired noise
of large leaves turning.

123

In greasy light
our godhead shines within us thinly.
Clothed in piercing sound
the granite fetishes
brood through sunken eyes.

Pieta

How strange that the gay body
with groaning anguish
should so suddenly be clay.
How strange — the liver's flaccid
and corpse cold — oh and heavy.

How strange that the mother
whose heart yearns, womb yearns, breast yearns...
forces tears from her own clay...
tears of water, tears of blood
in such pain...
and the astounded dust is puddled into clay
while she is fire of yearning, dust of longing.

How strange, the clay wells tears of water, gouts of blood
impatient to be dust,
and Mary with tears of anguish, gouts of yearning
compels him to be clay.
So she has his weight on her knee.
Mary from out her clay
has pressed the wells of yearning
and now is dust —
and Christ is clay.
So still they do not meet
and still she has him not.

War Museum — Royal College of Surgeons

This is the airman's heart.
He fell five hundred feet
and the impetus snapped the hurtling heart
from its two frail tubes.

And this is W.O. bottle ooo — a liver
with a large gash.
In spirit reposes!

And another bottle.
Six feet of small bowel
shot into pieces.
But he died of pneumonia.

And wax masks.
The speechless agony of shotaway faces
and pulpy tongues;
sweats blood, blood, blood...
quietly, with such pallor...
such dumb suffering
where no muscle remains to show feeling.

And here is stomach
with a large hole.
And another — very pale
which died of gas.
And many spinal cords clotted by fever.

Another — a chest clean open
like a basket of fruit
rotting in verdigris;
speckled purple and umber.
He too is a number.

Therefore for the unknown warrior
let us make a Christ
sweating blood but speechless.
With the open chest
the snapped heart
the gashed liver
and cutaway bowels,
the pale stomach that died of gas
and an obliterated face
that dribbles a tear from an eye corner.

Married

This roof tree holds us
with trembling darkness
and a thin murmur
and a feeling of moonlight.

In ferny odors
in shadow deep, deep
trembles the pale worm
in pulpy ambrosias of candle light.

Till he throws off his large cocoon
creeping small, small
through the wet darkness
and the feeling of moonlight.
Fearful she stiffens, then is fluid...
(O worm iridescent)
is absorbed, is transported
in sudden gyrations.

Disembowelled
he sinks shivering
clinging close, close...
but small and apart
and she warms him.

Permitted all, all...
and the clinging for comfort.
The tight blankets
and the long night
and the long morning.
The deep smells.

Out of the Water

Out of the water, the worm —
and dies;   and there is land:
and the soul swimming in dark
slimes its cocoon and dies:
but the body shifting in night
sets out its scaffolding rigid for an eternity

O leave it

But will not
fills it with mush
jelly that sweats and shuddering
speaks with a voice like madness

and dies

For glassy it holds in the light
which festers   eats in the bone

The skeleton   solid for an eternity
it speaks with a voice like madness

The Flying Banvards

How like a fish this woman in mid-air
Floats ere she whirls, teeth clenched upon a wire;
Taut body a new moon. Her hands respire
Like tadpole gills or hovering wings. Fair
Angel rapt and mute, quiring round what flare
Of Godhead, unsinged ever? while your shrill
Climbing hosannas strike out from the still
Void, sultriness as from Aghreb, rare
Sphere. The whiles your impotent male friends try
From springy asphodel to jump to sky,
But roughly tumble, fall with a cheap jest.
Alas! your wet secret raptures scattered
You come to earth. . . now I see your battered
Face and the ruined breast.

'Who thinks of Pensaers now?'

Who thinks of Pensaers now?
Yet I sat in cafés with him,
thought him intelligent when I got him pinned
admired his egyptology, as reported by Ezra,
and remember him in the island of the lake
of the Bois de Boulogne at lunch
with André and Madame V...
that fat bitch who bought a ring in Athens
with an intaglio of Leda and the Swan — too fine for her.
His speculations, remorse and wretched family,
poverty and a job he hated
his not-yet surrealist friends
turned his bile and he died like a dog in Brussels.

To a Renault in the Country

This car like a dolphin rolls down a wave of the downs
and the dark swirls like cloud in the beams of its eyes,
the trees shine green, such green, the hollow edge of a wave.
The rain splash bursts in the nose with a splash of salt.
Moths, caught in the storm, flutter, battling up in the light
like ships, and vanish in a waste which shudders, where rain
    flies in the void.
The earth smells of the sea, lightning etches trees on a pink
    sky,
then night, the shining abyss of tar, stinging rain.
The gravel crunches and sings, there is a low mutter and roar
    of shingle under the tide.

Lines to an Etruscan Tomb

Alive she lived in the dark warm wet of my heart
but moved towards light. Light took her apart.
She who was light was lost in light.
I should have fixed her in night.

But could not. Stone did. Here she lies
half leaning. I feel her hand. For her eyes
now wide on the dark I gave boys
girls boats and a plunging porpoise.

For a while, stone. She flying, then Death
caught her, he was grimmer, beneath
the dense unyielding stone
shoved in her rests with mine, bone on bone.

Havre Cathedral

Why are the flickering candles a crown of thorns
pale shining and trembling aspiring
pale in pale light
But the thorns dig in and are dark
dark thorn a drop, dark drop a ray,
each ray throbs light
pale round the bent head!

'Often a waitress...'

Often a waitress, tired at the end of a day
drags like a cow, her eyes ache, the roots of her hair
pull. You feel her blood thud at you everywhere
yet her head hangs, she seems to long to get away.
Thro all the mirrors, herself, each of her dishes
like each of her eyes, is a hundred reflected.
Tired or design, she brings a dish you rejected
her one little miracle of loaves and fishes.
Over the dumb voice of blood, the protesting eyes
flashes upwelling your long constricted rancour.
But startled you see, from her cocoon, emerging
she as she sees herself, soft, wanton, out surging
from each of her mirrors where you like an anchor
drag to the monstrous brew of all her breasts and thighs.

Adolphe 1920

ADOLPHE 1920

What had slit up his sleep? His eyes opened but the mind closed again. Piercing sweet the dawn star pierced him, his bowels shivering round it. On swooning mist and the far billowing of a lugubrious howl he swayed, till falling nearer, high bursting bubbles pulled him from his sleep. Morning lies round him. Behind the inn a bugle, in a far land heard before. A tent. A child skips, a trumpet to its mouth; a Moor throws up a ball. His soul fled after her through the cold light; snow falls, whirling...

Outside, clouds chase wildly over the sky and plunging into a rift, the star flies swiftly, gaily; and is swallowed in a sudden billowing of cloud.

In the wide street, under the bare trees, lorries; and in the drizzle a scattered crowd. A large white horse bumps round and round, a boy hanging to its cord. And still the dim lugubrious howl and rattling of bars.

Pent in cages, their choking burning smell makes a jungle round them. Tired, bored, they crouch in the dark vans, their very breath vitriol. Behind the bars, heads, teeth, eyes: lion or hyaena? A chattering monkey slobbers — Toms acold — and a negro, enormous, smiling, walks round the cages, a shovel smoking in his hands. Poles are going up, men are pulling guy ropes, an unwilling gaiety is being forced on the street.

Why do they go on living in the close cage, their bodies burnt through by the vitriol captivity distils in them. A man says I will die and dies; their breath, their dung, is poison, they will not die. And yesterday they were fifty miles to north, tomorrow will be fifty miles to south, and every day, day by day, the lions tents waxworks will be put up; that mob chase off in a frantic jingling of coins. Forever lions, waxworks, funny men, chasing through streets, the forests of hearts like trees lining road and pavement, the distance months, not miles, from the advance agent posting bills to the last dragging caravan.

Let him move off. He will meet that circus at Brives, Rocamadour, Figeac, Rodez, or else the bills announcing it, until by accident on some waste heath, he caught the flying Banvards come to earth.

> *How like a fish this woman in mid air*
> *Swims, teeth clenched upon a wire,*
> *Taut body a new moon, hands that respire...*

Himself. His wind-beaten, half legible placard still flapped on the walls of Claire, the city of Anne, the capital of Marjorie, the wide empty street of Angela. Let him turn out his lions, monkeys, blow his fanfare... What then? A girl would tiptoe round her cage with notes piercing sweet and wild. But if he dared look East, the sky lowers terror and dismay; or turning, the sun sets in fiery cloud, a rook belated, caws to its nest over watery meadows and black branches, filling him with grief and an echo, 'Winter and time to go now.'

The deserted city of booths, the morning wind, the sharp flap of canvas, drizzle, made him happy. Later Angela would come. When she saw the cages her eyes would fill with tears, but tomorrow she would forget. He turned from her with distaste. She forgot the cages endured by him for her, thought it right he should be perpetually with her, his bile burning through him hot and fetid as a beasts. He had no sympathy for himself, why then for them? They should be caged, they stood it worse, so he was avenged. And the time was long past since his beasts had done their tricks for her, and it was revenge had made him cage them.

She will cry in her room because of them. That will poison the air, make me think of her. I shall have to stop her. Her tears fall, and in me they are stones and rattle in my breast, but she is lighter without them. I must stop her. But I hate her. I have hated her from the moment our eyes first met. And never was a time that I left her but I said, I must never see her again, and something said Never? But how break? What letter write? Impossible! And if she comes for you? And her tears congeal about you like amber. And as if that were not enough, her tears speak to your tears, and they too flow in treacherous balm. Or she will write, and after some short silence you will answer. So you will go on tugging at that leash, till happens what you longed for but could not provoke, death or worse, a lover; then, amazed you cry: I was faithful. Young, I could not be faithful, that too would not work. Today, each thought a ruse, life proves me constant.

Now with a false trill, the roundabout wheezed loudly, battering cymbals, blaring trumpets, and wallowing in waves, dragon upon dragon rolled past, jaws yawning, light shimmering from iridescent scales.

The booths were now up, the cages hidden, the caravans drawn up in quiet streets, solid with trim doors, white steps and curtained windows; stranded vessels, their straying women shipyard figureheads.

A channel. The cold sea wind swept in over mud flats. Lurid green light pushed out of dark cloud. Darkness was falling, the gulls crying round the old boats, lit by an occasional warm light. 'Like Chrysomallo starting for her ride, joyously he had embarked on the enchanting possibilities of Angela, but that love which at first seemed frivolous and superficial, soon grew tenacious, tyrannical and full of torturing jealousy. The glaucous light shed from his spurs illumined the night, and was the symbol of that onward spurring love which no restraint could overcome and which inevitably must lead its victim into unknown fatal ways. It represented too, the penetrating and tragic effulgence which a grand passion must shed on all the sombre pages of an existence.'

Yes, and today that penetrating and tragic effulgence was a mist enshrouding him in corpse light: himself that unsleeping horseman whose accompanying shadow rose and fell with each hoof beat; while, to his mist-laden mind, in which bright objects moved and confused shadows, that shadow was denser than himself. Jabs and spots of scarlet rose and burst like moths about him, struck up by the flying hoofs. And once she had seemed hard and crystal clear but today he could not see her, and his incuriosity did not know what her shadow would do next.

Once he had known so clearly what she was, what her next act must be, and that he must not love her, so that after the first bright collision and repulsion, how soft, how wary had been his approach. Now for years she had come closer, till he could not see her. But if he went away he would see too clearly, till hysteria blinded him, dragged him back; yet if some effort more pronounced flung him from her orbit, could he support the bleakness suddenly before him.

The street was filling on all sides in a shuffling of feet, and from the booths like a twittering of birds rose the first timid cries of morning. And a sickly sweet smell of vanilla rose, cloying all the wet air, till some more violent blast from a passing woman washed it again. The road now lay between two rows of booths, where at intervals, stoves were frying potatoes in a sweet acrid smell of oil. All that like a crystal had grown about him since he awoke, and now part of it, drifting, he moved to and fro, half seeing but aware; his mind tall standards holding milky globes, a reverberation of deliberate feet on boards, faces drifting and featureless, pale in light, a sighing of sea, black close but unseen. And afterwards a tunnel, about him wild faces; and a cataract, an avalanche of light, twisting, twirling, a solid mass that bent his back and held him down; and, near, the crash and report of a car, leaping and falling along a switchback in a streak of light; a pale watery halo, a piercing scream of terror.

The shining nougat, ice cream and fritter stalls he saw now were nothing to the marzipan joints, sausages and edible offal which sweated there and were scarlet. All that light like a sky too near earth bent his back, and painfully his eyes were twisted earthwards.

The Marne at Nogent was better. The wet air was full of flying confetti, the street of clotted confetti, the river too. It filled the road, overflowed into stands, swept into dancing places. Canoes, racing eights, dinghies, moved on the flat gray river; among them, in and out, up and down, a water bicycle, solemn as an insect. Shouting burst when a heat flashed past, balloons climbed in the air, a plane swerved and darted, the landscape swarmed with insects buzzing round a bush in full summer. From the immense depths of sky mirrored in water, to the zenith, life swarmed.

That buzzing round a hive, that violent life of bursting cells was Angela, but when? Never the same, and every day he shook all up again, again to make the picture that would satisfy him. But he changed too, so it was all to do again. That bored him, he hated her. If he could get away he thought, and saw himself press her arm closely, affectionately, already hurt at her hurt. Near him a long shaking hand climbed into a house; and on it people ran, staggered, floated, slipped sometimes, and were carried up on their backs, kicking. Give him London, its escalators in thin light, himself dropping deeply in a solemn mutter and round him grave shades floating up and past.

Why did he want to go down and what would he do there? He was always running from what he did not know to what he could not tell. But others ran too, and in that wood, where bones and tusks litter the ground, the elephant casts a last look back. And if he too once got away, then he would fight to get back to Angela or some other, turn out his tricks.

Impossible not to desire in joyous anticipation his minute inventory by the pack, what trophies brought, what marks of what encounters. Hesitating he would come back. Tears welled in their eyes to see anything so savage, so distrustful. How he backed, his mournful dark eyes full on them, till wriggling nearer, tail wagging, in final paroxysm he turned his belly up in utter subjection for all to fall upon. But places too could hold him, he could make a new life. What kept St Anthony in his desert? Easier to stay than move! But how begin again and where? What keeps me here? And still he could not go. And even yet there was time but he could not, and with joyful expectation he went to the hotel to meet her.

But her telegram said forgive me cannot join you better so fond love angela.

Excellent he thought and sank into an immense cloud of relief. Now he could go where he would. Instead he felt very lonely and that the afternoon promised to be intolerable; and then suddenly his rage was too much and the thought of lunch sickening. And when, as though his eyes had deceived him he reread the message, he saw it came from Bordeaux.

That meant she was travelling. That meant she could not be alone. Such a storm of passionate jealousy and longing burst in him it left him exhausted. But how reach her and where? Yet he was glad she had betrayed him, glad she was as treacherous as sometimes he had thought her. Yet without the occasion, she might still be kind and true as any nut-brown maid. She would say it was because she loved she left him, to her that justified it. And Bordeaux, that was their place, a clean expressionless face where the Rue de Galles, that vein, half a heart, shut small doors, valves into close red rooms; the fat white all-eating leucocytes waited to give or take things from the blood, near by the oubliette of St Michael's. The mummies there were leather and she was leather. Their ragged skins sprang sharply back if the guide plucked a corner; the wagging heart was leather, the motheaten lungs were leather. For a hundred years a vapour casual and arsenic drove through that corner of the graveyard, pickling some thirty souls dead in 1600. Of all that town, all the preceding, the subsequent centuries, were dust. She too, some vapour had made hard, but not him. And when they met she would say it had to be for he had not truly loved her. Her life now seemed to him to be with them, lived in such a glimmering night, a giant marshal on her right, his breast thrust through; a shrinking mother on her left, squashed by earth, her baby tight upon her yielding shoulder like a pitcher; about her many pilgrim figures in shrouds, and rotting leg bones. And she, like them, now wore an apron of brown paper. All beneath was horror and decay. Hell, he muttered, climbing out of the crypt.

Lunch was a welcome break, but the slow service torture, afterwards he lit a cigar. First it would soothe, then sicken him; the oily cloud lubricate his thoughts, ease his mind of her. He went into the street. The smell of garlic and vanilla was violent, made his mouth water, tempted him to a second meal. He wondered could he eat again, wanted to, yet tore himself away. But then he thought it would be good to have a weight in his stomach and at the next stove ate mussels with relish, with nausea too and an anxious rapidity. The weight inside him got comfortably heavier and he sat watching the street, which slow oily and with sudden eddies loitered under a storm of beating drums, blaring cymbals, rattling mechanical pianos, noises of all kinds from boxes of all shapes. That shower on black water made the whole surface dance in rippling broken circles.

The beating air drummed new life into him, and himself again he entered the stream which opened and then held him. Now part of it, swirled eddying with it, afraid suddenly, he clutched a nearby stanchion. That man-eating one-leg stood sombre, with dark square eyes staring from its breast, waiting dumbly to be taken to others of its clan sunk like buoys throughout the street.

He slipped a penny into it. A warm light moistened its eyes, lit up its chest. He put his eyes on its eyes, his heart on its heart, listening deeply, anxiously; forgetting the fair, his fellows reading other hearts round him. But the excitement of beating air thrilled him, and the prospect of some approaching revelation made delay unendurable. It began to mutter. Where its heart was, a woman rose from a chair, smiled, patted her elaborate hair, unhooked a shoulder-of-mutton blouse, a petticoat or two, stood self-consciously for a minute in lace-edged drawers, laced boots and black stockings, smiling a timid 1890 smile. Wondering, fearful of losing it, he thought he could not bear her smile to fade, yet suddenly the eyes were dark, and he was with his thoughts. She too in that darkness, from which for a moment he had called her. A coin brought her back: as though gratefully she shyly reappeared, went through all her senseless gestures, smiled and smiled. And darkness again, heavy, inevitable. That room, that sofa, filled his brain with warm shapes and comforting light, and the woman moved amicably through it.

He turned away. Another creature in supplication held tentacles out to him, and when he slipped a coin into a dark hole in its side warbled and whispered. But he thought of Angela, and the heart he had just looked into made him loathe her and himself, and angrily he tore its tentacles from his ears, its lying words of love and bliss; wading from it into the watery flood, now swirling silently like an inundation. He walked on tiptoe, borne up by the tight mass, the corners of his eyes cut by the whirling flapping flags and pallid lights that filled the washed air.

In mid-air the endless band fluttered into the sky with its laughing staggering falling figures; above him flew boats with other figures; and on ostriches, pigs and in chamber-pots, flying wheeling crawling were still others. And the street was full of them, and the eating places; and their smell, vanilla urine garlic, blended, censing all in a vulgar sabbat.

Immutably the anthropophagi stood among them, a woman for a heart, tight round their secret lure for which no pain disease damnation were too much to pay. A woman walks in a room, she is alone and smiles, she seems a little mad; wears drawers and black boots, in 1890, and to the watcher all is miraculous. But his starting eyes touch glass. And behind, near, inferior, the talkers, singers; pensive, whispering if questioned. And on all sides large man-high boxes blaring a full orchestra. Through the wild gaiety of the severe machines, men moved distracted, their fun dark chambers, chutes, distorted visions, the agonies of nightmare.

Mad, they leapt, howled, sang, fought, forgot; carefully, minutely, went over each other; taking stock of teeth, eyes, hair; vibrated trembling, in a dry rattle of chitin, like ants, in love and epilepsy, before they leapt from each other. But to keep a man under his bowler, hundreds give their daily lives; the glands of half a thousand sheep nurse his beloved dropsical mate. Like madmen they were deaf to all but their own noises, yet their agglomeration was an intoxication to each.

In one head beats a surging sea, another hears distant bells, a third workshop machinery, a fourth is admonished by a defunct relative in dry rapid and unpleasant tones. The sickly incense of vanilla woven into these dreams is part of them, transfigured: and in each head strange shapes move, fiery coruscations.

His head ached. Mean of her to leave him. He hated the fair, yet if she were with him it would be fun. But the slow drive of the crowd dragged him. It began to seem he had never had any life but this. Yes, in a hut a girl tripped, a bugle to her mouth, but whichever way he looked all was darkness.... Like Chrysomallo.... But somewhere a heart lit up, a girl walked into the room. ... 1890 ... and the wild wet smell of snow. He hoped he would not be ill. All that food made him feel queer. He hoped it had been good. He did not know about mussels, his cousin died of typhus, sitting up, his eyes starting, dragging long ropes out of his throat. His head was turning. He wanted to push to the bank but could not. A wave of nausea rushed over him, but as he struggled out it left him.

And again he was in the crowd, moving with it like a leaf, seeming to turn upon himself, sink rise sink but with a continual gliding motion. As by some half drowned tree he was stopped by a dark clot round a booth. It was easier to go in. People stood loosely with cold eyes. A tired drab stole a moment there, a latchkey in her hand; two shop girls, white faced and with bright bandannas, seemed anxious to be going. In a cage a monkey crouched, shivering and shrunk upon itself, its eyes bloodshot and running, its jaws dribbling, its misery too human. The showwoman lifting the heavy snake from her neck replaced it. It hung from her like a badge of office. This ladies and gentleman is a boa-constrictor, he is changing his skin, hence the film over the eyes. Her eyes were a washed out blue, filmy. He changes his skin six to seven times a year during which he is blind. Aint you cocky. Deeply she looked in its eyes, warmed its jaws in her hand, then with a gesture indescribably caressing thrust them in her mouth. The audience, bored, began to move away. He went to her, asked her how long they lived, to what size grew. She did not know. He was her pet, and oh, she loved him, was inseparable from him. Astonished he asked himself what lay behind the tired face, the defiant jargon; her gesture had been different. The world suddenly held too many problems, too much that needed explanation. Her gesture held him with snake-like fascination. He knew he must see her again, asked might he take her out. She didnt mind if he did, but having to perform each fifteen minutes, could not be free till midnight. He said he would call back.

The filmy eyes considered him. She would be very tired. But she was tired now and it needed too much energy to refuse. The next performance must begin and if she did not say yes, he might perhaps not let her give her mind to it. Yet, if she were too tired she need not go, and it was possible as sometimes happened that midnight might revive her.

He went away. He too was very tired, but all that had taken his mind off Angela. His mouth was bitter with a taste of death. He had stood too long in the crypt of St Michaels. For days, for weeks sometimes, that taste rose in his mouth, poisoning his thoughts, his feeling for his friends, a foretaste of death and putrefaction. His shoulders bent, he wrapped his coat tighter, thinking with despair that Angela was warm, but that the future still held something for him, since he would see again that bleareyed loose-featured woman.

And again he flung himself into the dark swirling flood, sinking rising sinking with a continual gliding motion.

He felt his arm seized, and when he turned his head, saw Monica. Fighting, they struggled to each other, enchanted by the encounter, and fearful of being separated, clung together. O I was looking for you she said, but I couldnt believe I should find you in all this. He was looking at her. She was the same, older, but not changed. He wondered, thinking she was too glad to see him, that she seemed to have too much to say to him, too much; and that he did not mean to give her the opportunity, for there was too much on his own mind. Yet if he asked himself what he thought, there was nothing but his brain thudding Bordeaux, Bordeaux, round a flat picture of the Rue de Galles, the glassy empty aquarium of the Chapon Fin, the long dark wharves and warm cafés. If Monica spoke, the whirring screw ran down for a moment with a sigh, and easily he answered her, but in the following silence that word again began to turn, slowly at first, then bewilderingly fast, an obsession. He looked at her and her features and clear smile warmed him, but he knew her too well, and she could not comfort him. For a moment, for an hour, he might lose himself in her, but tragically, remorsefully; and though she would forgive him his turpitude, sublimating it perhaps, or accepting his trivial balm, he would not be able to forgive himself. But it was not forgiveness, it was rather that she forgot. They all forgot, clinging to some bias or invention, following blindly, a gazelle pursuing the receding hunter. Curiosity was born with the universe so she would follow. Not devotion, but in dark night, in crooked gloom, up creaking stairs, a woman follows a man she has never seen. That made existence impossible. He behaved well that he might not reproach himself later, but they forgot everything, the good, the bad, kindness, cruelty. And if he thought himself kind they saw it cruel, or if outraging himself he grew cruel, he made a devoted mate. That destroyed everything, made all things possible in a sentimental relation, made nothing worth doing. His own feelings then must be his final criterion, for they would be sure to find some talisman, rock of ages, interpretation, to which to cling in hypnotic stupor. That meant he must walk in his own dream as he now walked, and the cobbled space in which he found himself was a stupor too.

In the middle of this tent where a few workmen, soldiers, servant girls, moved uncertainly over the wet black cobbles and among the exhibits, Snow-White lay sleeping; her breast rising and falling with a strained mechanical regularity, and at too similar intervals the eyelids fluttered up and then closed. Leaning, they peered into the glass bier, but the bright blue eyes were empty, the parted lips unmoving. In the bleak tent she was a patch of light, of snow, so the tent seemed darker. And in the dark tent the unnatural waxy bloom of her hands and features was a leprosy, blanched, scaling, aromatic. That sickened him, he pulled Monica away. Horror on horror, waxy, sweating, gashed, on all sides were dead chunks of flesh on which some livid parasite bloomed and spread, the scarlet ropes and strings of half a pinched ascetic face, a thorax spilling all its fruit in rotting tropical brilliance, greens, speckled purples and umbers. And in the gloom that smelt of mould, a tray, an egg, the egg dividing, dividing again, budding, growing, hollowing itself, mad to begin its life, and ending round, pitted, a golf ball. But not lost, carried then to the wall cases, injected into the seven wombs, growing still, larger, involuting, adding a cord, hanging, the flesh yielding in livid wax sprinkled with sparse discoloured hairs. Soldiers, shopgirls, workmen, stared wondering at shapes they could not know, unmeaning to them, viscera, a sheep's pluck merely. Life to them was skin, hair, eyes, teeth; such they knew themselves, such were their friends. And a man smelling of mould moved among them dusting cases. Yes, yes, he thought, life held too many problems. Madness. We wore our clothes, sweated, held each other by the hand, about us the flesh grew, swelled, collapsed; gave us prodigies, diseases. This lump from out the ambient air found some demon to inhabit it, guide it through the dangers that beset its blindness. But suddenly mute and evil began to turn against its demon, trying in despite to fix itself. To catch what sombre vibration did the ear begin to turn to stone, the eye turn stone, the nails grow stone, and stone settle in the brain and in the bladder. The riddle is set thus; Take a skeleton. Make it solid. Admirable foundation, might last any time. Fill its holes with brain eyes bowels lungs; give it wires with which to move itself and lap all round with skin. Content, it adds atom to atom; but full, settles stone in the soft mush. Then the heart gives a last convulsive leap, flutters; the eyes fall in, how ragged the orbit seems, the limbs tremble, for a long time the skin twiches. Shatteringly the bones fall, the demon flies far far. Some other blind insensate frame will house him.

What word of enchantment made that thing move? What word joined wheel to wheel? Yet while he lived in it, how sweet his sojourn, how eagerly obeyed him, gave such rapture. And that brain ran flew dived, no realm too far, no province too divine. Yet objects moved in it and shadows, and itself leapt to and fro weaving memorable dreams. Some brains do that too often or too much, a firework turning on itself, coruscating light; till suddenly it falls, bursts everywhere, and leaping to and fro spends itself in anguish and dismay. Such is the bone's madness. Its thoughts eternal but too old. Its face is like our own but heavier, coarser, and speaks loudly. Soft and sweet the mushes' thoughts run, but fever heat or cold will interject that stony finger, turn them dashing into wastes of sand and arid stone where snakes live, and offspring of the djinn.

It was impossible to stay but Monica would not leave. She darted about with solemn cluckings and round ecstatic eyes. He wished he had not met her, he might have been out. His patience was an intolerable burden, weighing on his shoulders, and his stomach ached dully. The tent grew smaller, stifling. Moodily he leant upon a case, seeing her stop at a twin fœtus oozing straw into its bottle, then at the speechless agony of a shot-away face dribbling a tear from the corner of an eye, tongues like slabs of liver, an airman's heart snapped from its two frail tubes in some vertiginous fall, six feet of small bowel shot into pieces, her astonishment and rapture growing at each step. That revolted him and the cold was in his boots. And he was frightened, feeling he had come upon some mystery, where like a novice she waited for the flesh to open, hear its awful accents thrill the air, hear its blood speak to her blood. He took her arm tightly, moving to the door. In his path a man stood and in his arms a minute creature in a dinner suit. The midget held a top hat out and when he dropped a coin thanked him with a deep startling voice. Its tiny face was severe, contracted, its chin blue with shaving. Stood down, for a moment its insolence deserted it, but frightened, ashamed, large enough for bravado, it put a hand out dragging him down to itself. Not however without continual apprehensive glances as though some careless child might tread it underfoot. Lifted up it smiled again, waved its hand and went out gaily. Filthy. As though its innumerable generations had been handled by hordes of sweating men, their greasy thumb-prints marked it still, its stature unfit for our larger virtues. There was a man once, so wretched he was the slave of dwarfs. His bites were meals to them, his clothes would need one of their tents, his eight-hour sleep an age through which two of their cycles ran, and twice therein must they be roused and fed and cleaned and put to bed. Small wonder soon he grew brutish as they. It was much older than himself. That was too much. Its life so circumscribed, its need to live so fierce, ten of its lives might be encompassed by his own. Ten times nearer death he thought with satisfaction, clenching his teeth upon the thing whose tenacious look was prehistoric.

In the booth the half light was thick in the corners and under the cases. The air was throbbing into afternoon, the frames wavered in it, and their waxy contents vibrated and lived. And the air trembled and lived too, and a vague population flitted batlike from the walls so that the air was full of it. Solemn faces shuffled from behind cases, disappeared, their faces swimming into wax. The wax rose and lived and the life of the place ebbed and flowed on a deep stertorous breath. The shimmer of darkening air confused his eyes, made them water. Blind wings were beating his head, his own being was confused and tenuous and his mind was ceasing to think. He too vibrated to the life of the place. His lethargy, the lethargy of all who now stood in the tent, alarmed Monica, and frightened, feeling she was trapped, she seized his arm and dragged him into the air. He was still at peace and his last vibrations faded in the street. The light was leaving the sky. The lamps had a bright dewy look, the air was brighter, thinner; the movement slowed, was loitering, as though all nature expected some shrill call to echo down the street, tear the air to brighter tatters, deliver an awaited message. There was a thudding in his ears. He thought it was the silence and his heart, but it was a steam engine generating power. His mouth seemed full of blood and in his nostrils was a smell of mould. And suddenly high and very clear there was the evening star in the pale sky. How could time pass so quickly. He had thought his every moment so significant, how could he lose a second. Into what blank caves was it pouring? Monica was looking at him with parted lips. He bent towards her. Her lips touched his own. So taut with blood they were, they trembled on his own, their dryness clung to his own dry lips, sticky as sundew. So hot, so full they were, her heart throbbed through them, through him, and blindly tightened his arms about her. She was trembling, her eyes beginning to turn up and all her weight heavy upon him. That brought him hastily to and he pushed her away, began to walk on. But she walked with him, clutching at his arm, his wrist, his elbow, finally his fingers, kneading and pressing them, her fingers anguished and so charged, the heart throbbed through them, such passion of longing sent from her to him he pulled his hand sharply away, turning from her. What could she want of him and he had known she had too much to say?

The street was full again about him. As though deceived the weary stream flowed gently, the noise and lights but half assured, but in so many eddies his gait was troubled and he was pushed from group to group. He was sick of Monica and tried to hide, glueing himself to a machine, furtively pushing a coin into its side. It lit up gratefully for him. There was a strange cottage in tender colouring like a lustre jug, with clipped trees in the garden and a man laughing at him, and then a shriek and a man and woman rushed into the house, the first man after them. He was afraid, and a gasping head burst out of a window with another head biting into its neck, the man and woman popping suddenly out of windows on either side. Gaiety and then a sense of fear, and after, deep terror. He gasped, half shrieked, and sudden sweat congealed in his armpits. And darkness fell on his eyes swift as a shutting hand.

The street now frightened him. He dared not trust his thoughts. However pleasantly he started them at any moment they might hurtle to and fro, weaving memorable dreams. How could he trust himself to think when dismay watched him from every corner. And the street was ghastly: white faces with revulsed eyes under the lamps. And while he looked at them, suddenly as though by enchantment, the crowd seemed tired of waiting, the faces opened and began to glide away, a cataract of noise burst over him, incense of garlic and vanilla climbed into the sky. He was very tired. He would go back and rest.

He lay on the bed, burying his head in the pillow, as though to shut out that torturing presence, stuffing his mouth to stifle the brain that cried out for her, but his will had left him, wrapped tightly about her, and his muscles, now a mush, trembled in vehement agitation which grew in violence, terrifying him. That passed into stupor, in which he grew stronger, till again his muscles trembled fearfully in agitation, the bed shaking under him, his breath caught with pain by the stopped heart clutched in a cold hand. He must have fallen asleep.

What was he dreaming. He remembered he had awakened moaning. Ah, he had fallen to the ground weeping, gnashing his teeth. But what? Angela! The time she was with him and he was trying to say: I cant stand you. You must go. But he could not and as in life he could not. Conscious of all he did, thinking he was acting, he had fallen to the ground, noises bursting from his dreaming throat. Go away, I cant bear you, you are killing me. She began to look frightened, then pleased, and he was glad he had been able to say it at last, that she had understood. His moans had wakened him but he must have fallen asleep again for his hands were joined and he had just been counting his fingers. One two three four five, four three two, they were all right. He awoke, the room was darker.

But it was no colder so he could not have slept long. His booted feet were too heavy on the bed and his overcoat embarrassed him. The air vibrated from the buff paint of the walls and bands of light fled low under the ceiling like a maze of flies. The loud noise of the fair reverberated in the room and the hotel swayed to it. But more important was the scratching at the door and the softly turning handle. Half bemused by sleep, he was afraid, then anxious. He saw Monica walk to his bed and sit beside him, her heart throbbing into the room.

How can you hate me so?

What could he say to that? Nothing in two words and longer would be intolerable.

You will not see me, you avoid me.

How mournful that made the room and her voice came from far away.

He avoided her and her life ebbed to some other star. Her voice came back, put out appealing hands.

What have I done to you?

How cold his feet were and his overcoat embarrassed him and her voice buffeted him.

Of course you love Angela, but why do you hate me?

Every moment made it more difficult for him to begin to talk, to explain. That made him sulky.

I never stood in your way. I helped you to her. She was my friend first. You met in my house. He wanted to get up, move, gesticulate, explain, comfort her, bring back the features to the pallid receding mask, but the room was too small and his feet were cold and her voice buffeted him.

The atoms danced in the room, confusing him.

Listen Dick, it isnt much Im asking. Let us be friends. Cant you see youre behaving badly. People are sorry for me and Im beginning to be sorry for myself. I shall begin to have a grudge against you and I dont want that.

That upset him. I dont want your magnanimity. Hate me if you want. I cant keep up with you. Ive told you often, so everythings impossible.

But I cant hate you, I wont! she cried. Why should I? Cant I see you sometimes?

Yes, but then!

O but I shant ask anything more, only do let us be friends. Ive been so miserable without you. I behave stupidly too. She was crying. He didnt know what she wanted. It was easier to let her cry. She was talking through her tears. What is the matter with me anyway. I cant sleep. Im afraid to go to bed, and my heads full of you. I read for hours till my eyes cant bear it and theres always you between me and the page. And if I do fall asleep I wake at five or six with such a taste that lifes impossible, then I get up and rush round the house, doing things. And all the time Im crying stupidly; it doesnt hurt, only I just cant stop. It doesnt mean anything Dick, but do let us be friends. I dont know what I feel for you, if its love or affection, but a lot of my life was bound up in you and if I dont see you I cant feel easy. I wonder about you and what you are doing. And I get jealous of you too if I dont see you. Whereas, if Angy were here now, it would be all right. We are friends and you couldnt come between us. I assure you she is more jealous of me than I am of her.

The thin voice prattled on into the dark, the face grew darker, more remote, and still he had no word to bring her back from that far gloom into which she seemed fast vanishing. Like a turning wheel, spokes of light poured into the wardrobe mirror, spouting into a dark cavern, its throbbing bosom lighting, darkening, the suffering mask floating upon its gasping surface, and like Ophelia her words were light and dark too.

It is a kind of madness, like my tears which flow so easily, my mind must think of you. I thought at first I might be going mad. Now its so much part of me I dont notice it. She laughed shudderingly. Thats very funny. And only sometimes and for no reason my thoughts catch some snag and then it hurts, everything hurts. Please dont think I think its your fault, its how Im made. And I was fond of Angy and she liked me too. Its mean of her to hate me. That makes me furious sometimes. She put out an ingratiating hand.

What a bore I am. Ill stop in a minute. Thats the difficulty you see. I get started and then its hard to stop. Tears words thoughts, everything all so mixed. And if theyre nice to me I howl, cant stop myself. She laughed again, her voice a suppressed exhausted shriek. He half lifted himself to go to her but she started away, no dont touch me, and sank again into the dark. O how miserable I am, and then savagely, but why turn her against me. You know I was fond of her and she of me. That makes me mad with you. O cant you understand, and drily to herself.... Yes I know Im repeating myself.

He could not understand how she came to be telling him all this. Surely he heard her but that was not her meaning and heavily her proximity weighed upon him. He had loved, he loved no longer. It was a story read in a book, and herself, her features, were outside him, and outside him the voice that once like the purring gaslight sussurated in his ears long after their meetings. Yet her misery needed comfort and to make some sincerity in him he tried to remember her and what he had loved in her, but her limbs, her eyes were vague... he had forgotten them. Yet he could not utterly have forgotten her, some intolerance still stayed, else sympathy must well up in him, his heart go out to comfort her, find the word to say. There was a wall between them. Then he must hate her. No, for then he should want to humiliate himself, taking her. He did not want that either.

Then it was all nothing. Nothing to say, to do, their past tenderness this annihilation. The room grew darker. In the impossible situation he found he had risen, saying with cold fury, dont fuss now about Angela, she has left me. He hoped that might bring her to herself: it jerked her to her feet, a hand clutching at her heart: she whispered: O then I shant see her any more. And that too he thought coldly was not her, not what she meant, and angrily he went from the room; but in the passage he was suddenly sorry and went back. He opened the door and the room that had seemed all silent was full of a clamour of shouting and mechanical noise, and at intervals deliberate spokes of light streamed over his face into the mirror. Below him, very far, very small, on a white square, the woman lay huddled. Such a fumbling effort to get to her, he could hardly undertake it. And that made her false, seem acting, and warily he sat by her. She did not move. She lay in a caul of dark throbbing sound and spokes of light flew over them like a maze of flies. Blankly and as though that was her life she lay till he should return with some life giving sound. He pushed a wary hand under her waist, found a cold wrist. She did not move. But soon some grateful glow flowed through to him. The room that held her seemed to grow more light, she stood up, smiled, caressing moved towards him. He bent his head. Still she came to him, growing larger, warmer, overwhelming him. He could not breathe.

She had turned round. Her warm arms were round his neck, her wet lips on his own. He wanted to cry out but could not, wanted to rise but could not. He was pulled down into darkness.

Snow was falling, flurrying round him and he shut up with it. Why did she shake him. He wanted it to settle so that he could look into his heart which

145

was dark and oppressive, but comforting because of its weight. His being throbbed painfully. The hour was turning hodden gray.

He was inside outside a plate glass window, icy, glacial. His friend was by his side. A spire went up into the sky and near him a stove crackled. His face was warm, his back was cold. They were alone and snow was falling, flurrying round them, melting.

His eyes pricked with acid tears which etched frail paths of light. With an immense effort he pulled himself from her, pulled her to him. We must go out. The effort was too much for her and swaying, she stood up, leaning heavily upon him. He led her into the street. The noise fell away. He was dragging a dark monster heavily after him. In a sudden press of the crowd he slipped her.

The sky was woolly, mole gray, but one lurid bar of orange still lingered. That seemed better. He breathed again but his mind was gray, his being gray and continually he thought, the hour turned hodden gray. His skin pricked, it had swollen, touched his clothes at all points. That exposed too much, made him shiver, the crowd was no protection. He slipped from that too, walking down a long street. There were lamps high up but the street was dark. Like a dog, he came gratefully into their field, reluctantly left them, a minute point of gaiety at each encounter. But sometimes light would surge up and move past him from a slow clanging tram, leaving him more alone. He thought of Angela in the dark crypt, but all was horror and decay. With loathing he felt the street too long for him, knew he must go back to the crowd. He thought he would begin to drink.

That tightened his mouth and throat in a spasm of nausea, then he felt warmer. It was as though his own eyes lit up, his own heart began to mutter, and with excitement he longed for someone to gaze into him. Glassily the street reflected itself in him, unseeing he walked through it. His body shrank again, his clothes lapped him more comfortably round. An interior gaiety filled him and bubbling over, insalivated, made gay and digestible whatever he might look at.

O but where was she? He loved her but she did not love him. She was far away and he was shrunk into himself, but not unhappily. Yet he must go to her for that would focus all his thoughts. But where find courage? If he could so resolve, his mind would stop till the train left, till he got to Bordeaux even. Yes, but how try the hotels and what name ask for? And if he met them she would look incredulous and then what, heavens what? He would not imagine it, he was afraid his heart would suffocate him. And if he did not find her, to know her happy and near him was more than he could stand. He must put up with it. His turn now. He too had pushed a rival out. This was as inevitable. He was not complaining. But she only of the two was hard, and where could he find a vapour to tan him. But she was soft too, softer than himself and she never knew when things were ended. She would come back pretending fear, sure she could have him. And if he sent her away she would

146

wail, want to kill herself. She would always have her way, always have the last word. And if by some impulsive movement ever so little out of hand, she killed herself, that too was a last word. As though he played. Beginners luck; the counters heaped in front of him, other players pushed out yet pacing the bright room that was such gloom to them, their nerves on edge for dawn to tear them away. And going out, if a drawn face looked a wistful question, he would turn. How could he know, he would not know, that grimace was fear, his own grimace perhaps; that out of the night of obsession a sudden spark might touch off death to be where life was, a moment destroy eternity. His fault? In anguish he denied, yet rather that and his refusal willed than that a sudden jerk should rob him of the tribute of her act. Why had her look not said, why had she not said? His blindness was not willed. His heart was pounding. She could not save herself, even now was wretched, and he could not get to her, protect, assuage. The blood rushed to his face, his breast. Yet nothing could happen to her. In the blindness of her intoxication she must always fall soft. They had got to Camomile. Who said that women, despite themselves, before they notice, have reduced to camomile all love that starts champagne. It was too true, and stupidly he had thought it was himself slowed down their love with thinking, now its settling into what I want. No more late nights, peace only, friendship. Yet despite herself and conscious she herself had changed that brew, she thought it was the story of the horse. He had got her down to but one straw a day. That was too little or too much. She must have saved that up against him for some time. Now the old short cycle of her life would begin again as so often before. The intoxication of love, wine, moony nights, talk and talk and a new face opposite her, remote, flying, to be pursued, drowning her in words till gasping she could come up again and cling to it.

What was his prose to her? Of course he loved. She knew it and was grateful, but that was not it.

The truth was he was bored with late nights. He did not want to drink and he had used all his tricks. When he was drunk he heard the clock, and she was that clock, ticking away his life, nothing, nothing; and if he did not remember what he had said, he was ashamed. But it was then her mind took wings, her anaesthesias weakened, her thoughts lived with darting presences, a host of faces came to their board speaking through her, mimicking, grimacing, alien. And there were dead among them.

But the population inside him had mournfully withdrawn, veiling its face. In drink she melted like the fabled pearl that does not melt, giving herself in a glass.

That too he had borne... and been patient. Then all was gone, the alien voices silent, the heaving breast, moist warm eyes, gone too, all all exorcised: comfortable peace lapped him round and he flattered himself her too.

And she had liked it, no doubt wanted it, had meant to go on with it as he had meant to go on with it, but one day some new far face had drawn her off, the creatures inside her clamouring in chase, maddening her to spill them after him, their violence too much for her, she helpless, able only to watch her quarry torn by them, like Circe, be as beastly as those she made bestial.

All that intoxication of the chase again and again to be racked by remorse for what she had left. It was too strong for her, it was her life. But now he waited for her, they met each other half way. She felt his hesitation and herself hesitated. Another had known better how to act as he had once known how to act. And he envied her bitterly, wanting to force a new love to himself, but knew he dared not undertake it, had not her blind courage; yet he would have been glad to find himself suddenly and as though against his will barely struggling in some new sea of love or its illusion; his problem stilled a while. Alone he could not effect that monstrous effort. Easier to stay where he was or go back. Yet he knew how bitterly he would hate being back, as though a child again and the intervening years which justified him annihilated. How love had made him love love. Such a business, the first years of adolescence; like drink, something to make a man of him. Now let him try to cast it off. And he thought it strange that he should still be glad when he did not see her, and strange that he thought a month would see him over it.

Why did he not force her back as he had once forced her to him. She would be grateful to have no more problems, perhaps longed for him now to rescue her from the morass of doubt and miasmas of past love her new love could not but evoke. He saw her fallen under the pack, helpless, wide eyed, it was tearing her too. But he could not go to Bordeaux. He knew he could not face her indignation and even if she wanted him, that would be her impulse. And he would have nothing to say to her and there was no appeal could touch her; he had lost the right to force her, had forgotten how.

He had walked back towards the fair and now found himself on the edge of a crowd round a wooden platform level with his eyes. There was a bear on it and a fat wrestler and a thin wrestler. And a large woman in gray shorts. And a flour-white-faced boy with heavy eyes. And a clown, red blotchy and with red eyes. And a dog squatting on the newel post and a woman at the cash desk. And yet they managed to pass each other, dance a little, shake hands, handle weights and stand on their heads. And the clown cried out in a plaintive voice, side splittingly. That made him realise he was sobering, he thought he would go away, but the drum stopped beating and the crowd surged up the stairs and into the tent, taking him with it. A fat and thin man were wrestling. They sparred deliberately, like lovers fell wantonly and lazily upon each other with laughing eyes and red hanging tongues. They sought out each others weaknesses, but both were weak, and head on hand and elbow on the ground, for long minutes they meditated gravely upon each others rumps shoulders arms and legs. That was exquisitely funny. But if one attempted some coup it was promptly countered; then both were still. That was like himself and Angela. Why didnt they move, do something. How mournful his life was.

But the woman came in. She pushed the fat man out of the way, wrestled and fell heavily upon the other. What had been tranquil, amusing, was now strenuous and upsetting. It pulled him together, his heart began to race, he was excited but furious too, for the third person filled his mouth with bile. It was bad enough to make contacts with one person, that took time and patience, eventually it might work; but let a third in and the mean level changes, for a long time there is chaos, a tyranny of new standards, compromise at a new level or the annihilation of the preceding effort. For even the accustomed act demands an effort of the will; and that love which flowed from him, despite himself he thought, and whose inarticulate existence must in itself convince, did so; but one day he went blank, let go; and she whose life lived only for and round him thereafter lived about another, a circle to shut him out. Yet sometimes drink or night would wake her, cut that caul; she lived another older life; the hand goes hard up to the terrified mouth, O God, it is not Dick!

The show was not funny now. It began to be sad, even tragic. The woman went through it like a whirlwind. First she settled the fat man, then the thin one, finally the bear. She only was victorious. That disgusted him, he gave in too, leaving the tent. And again was surprised and confused by the noise, the flashing lights of the fair, the deep excited hum which throbbed through the street. He fell so easily into his own dreams, he had forgotten the life that raged outside him, the loitering black stream. What should he do next? So many side shows...all boring....Shoot perhaps? Or throw a ball....Such an effort.

He moved slowly with the crowd, supported by it. Heads and napes of necks moved with him, always the same. But before he knew his heart turned over, pounding, and blood rushed to his face and shoulders. He stood swaying, thought he saw the face he looked for, made off after it. The loitering crowd checked him. Sidestepping, pushing, he followed and could not come close. That presence fled before him and his heart thumped loudly and sweat dried on his face. He thought she knew he was following for when he came near she turned with a look of annoyance, then slipped rapidly into the opposing stream. It was difficult to leave one for the other and she was far away; dodging elbowing, he came up with her, but with a sudden flirt of the body she turned and slipped out of the stream. He followed, found himself in a backwash of sleeping caravans. In the sudden stillness he forgot his object, wandering aimlessly in the deserted street, but then his loneliness was too much and he went back to the crowd feeling his heart too heavy, musing sadly could it have been Angela, what was she doing there and had she meant to cut him; or was it some other creature vaguely remembered, who having known him now avoided him, or someone who had forgotten him, or one unconscious of him, her quickness merely impulsive; or again he had been tricked by some puff of scent.

O but if it had been Angela how different his life might be. And the evening which now hung so heavily upon him might instead be bright and dewy.

On ne revient jamais. He thinks one day he sees her on the street, his mouth smiles, his eyes fill, and see in that mean cherished object the thing he loved. And finds he yearns for what was sometimes hell, for in his mind the thrush still sings there all the day, at night the frogs croak loudly to each other. But why round her? He thinks of frogs in lands 3000 miles away and is as moved.

Their tops once younger, what moved them towards each other. Now they stand back. No power can bend them nearer but their roots are crabbed and wind about each other still. And that bowed head, so simple and so mean, that no one else picks up, can turn from him; he sees it go and yearns to follow; his impotence hurts him.

He had drifted out of the street and pouring light and saw it was night again. There were stars in the sky and a bright haze of cloud or stars over him. Here and there from marquees in uneven hollows a golden glow trembled into the sky. Paraffin flares blazed smoked spluttered at each door, pouring a pale light of despair on the black knots of people huddled in anxiety scanning the sky. He too joined them. For a moment he felt it would rain hail and fire, that he would be beaten to pieces with thunder and lightning. He made an effort, recovered himself. Nearby a rattling organ jerked fictitious life into him, and into soldiers in pale blue who danced two by two with drawn twitching faces and sunken eyes, clutching at each other sometimes to belch a superflux of liquor.

He was afraid of the stumbling forms, afraid of the dark and the vast hysterical canopy of noise that hung upon him, muffling his head in its folds, flapping confusingly round him, and pushed into a tent, sat at a table, became one of a thousand pink faces mumbling in a noise of shouting, crockery, his mind jagged with flashing white sleeves of waitresses. He sat there for a long time: no one came. He sank into his own thoughts as they must be sunk in theirs. Fire and hail, sin, repentance, the devil, what? A sort of menagerie each carried inside himself. How heavy the head must be with the slow tortured forms that move in it. Dark as night, some loathsome iridescent edge to catch the light.

Years had passed too quickly. He had nothing to show for them, and it was as though she, like Aaron's rod, had engulfed the minor years preceding her in his life, and like that ungrateful snake become a rod again, sapless and with no buds. His years had disappeared into her and there was nothing to show for them. And when he looked within himself asking what she had given him there too was nothing. Perhaps he had been too heavy and she had taken what might hamper him, a drone, leaving his bowels inside her? Yet he did not feel lighter and his life was unendurably heavy.

Years had passed. Like a funnel she had hung over him, sheltering him, piously collecting all his exhalations. That he had thought to be love. But it was because she was empty and lest air should crush her. He might tell her she had deceived him. It was bitterly cold without the protecting funnel for his fermentation blew him out, there was too much skin, he was too exposed. But that would be untrue. Security then, the illusion of which she had given him, that had deceived him. No, for he had always suspected it. What had he then against her. Nothing. It was himself had deluded himself. And whereas before he knew her he had resented and feared her for reasons which he could have defined, now he could not see her and there was no definition adequate to her. For her generosity was her body's, her greed or love the impossibility of being alone, her weakness a cozening, and undermining, not of the strongest, but harder still, a moles burrowing under the weak, and he got what he wanted of her because no other wanted it more.

What was he in all that and what had he expected. She lived in the past yet her eyes were fixed in the future. Her intoxications came from the future yet she sobered quickly. The future had barely time to exist for her before it became the present and the past. He dined with her, and trembling and in tears, she could not tear herself from the past; thus his wretched predecessor must come for her, take her to a ball where she will find a lover, now happily tranquil, from a ten years past. Like a loathsome, but tortured puzzled Hecate, she kept her loves inside her. They dropped from her or she dropped them and thought with sadness and relief, thats over, but their beings still mingled with her being, their thoughts were still her thoughts, and like the princess of the Arabian nights her lusts were theirs more than her own. Yes, so that made her simple or sick, the weak ape thrilled in anguish before its bullying senior, the epileptic in erotic swoon when the beloved doctor approaches.

When all that spilled over him, it filled his mouth with bile, his brain with furious reverberations. He was that horse in the city of dead whose hoofs paddled, whose gait was tangled in sweet smelling plague struck entrails. He could have wished her to cry out at such periods as did her savage sisters; warning him not to cross her path; but she seemed unaware that anything was happening. Her face might light up even but their coming and going did not stir her. And afterwards the silence was doubly mournful, the hour was hodden gray, she wondered what had upset him. She had forgotten them and when the time came for him to cease writing, his successor would be as miserably occupied in comforting her as he had been. Then she would forget him too. Merciful forgetfulness, how much she had to be grateful to it.

But did he not forget too?

They stood drinking, their bark drifting, eyes in eyes; and though he knew the philtre good for three years only yet he drank to that eternity, knowing its first glow would be omniscience of her and her love, all close within his palm. His birds glance felt it could foresee, meet, unravel, all the unwilling wiles her doubts, her love must force upon her; he could protect her from herself and solid meet each shock. The years would pass, the drug thin, his frightful fervour too, and his velleities stronger grown make her seem vague, deep under sand. He had forgotten her, could not know what she would do, his impotence bewildering him. Yet his life seemed stable to her and what she drew from him made her stronger though the drug faded through the long years, longer grown. And Mark, old, had got his rights and cold they lay beside each other. So he lost her and his blood poured a new philtre in his veins. Alone, his frightful fervour raging, he can again protect, assuage, foresee, but what? And all their phrases, once all fire, burn, make the blood rush and the heart beat. And where was either? Hardly can some reverberation wake them where they lie in deep tombs of themselves, but half unwitting the heart still leaps to an accustomed bell in a far other land, or to the slammed door of a cab though no one comes or to curtains fluttering in a window which knows her not or he will be alone in dark Ravenna where half guessed frogs hop round Dantes tomb.

Yet now, if a creature, half devoured, attempted to escape, leaving an ice of loneliness to freeze inside her, a last warm glow lights the mournful eyes, the fluttering appealing hands cling, cajole, hold it back, restore its shivering confidence till they can thrust it back again and forget it.

Yet there were creatures like him who had got out. She spoke wonderingly of it. Some took a fortnight, a month, or one sombre meeting was enough. In a close room, on the lagoons, a cat leaps from the tumbled bed; sudden rape in a rocking train. Then harsh words or a letter, or nothing, and all was over. She wept or her eyes were furious, or it was well; but for a moment, her self-love shuddered. What gift helped them, what knowledge told them she was sterile? What native integrity held them from being the slave of a slave, slave of each contact; her buying, seeing, hearing, doing. It ate her life and a thin excitement made it worth living. So she was slave to love, which she imagined slave to her because her heart only was in it; so always it must be begun again. She was unchanging, so they must bend. And some were glad to drown themselves in her and what she was slave to, some went half way, and some violently attracted, as violently recoiled. And when, in years they met, they were in love with love, the misunderstanding vanished, recalling how it was the best time of their lives. Smiling in an anxious effort of memory she agreed.

Yet had he been ever so little more impulsive he too would have been free long long ago like those he envied, but impossible for him to make that gesture. If he were simple, avoided scenes, he might watch the daily disintegration of their love, two roots turning naturally away to other wider fields of aliment, unless, crabbed, they wound about each other, crippling, destroying. Often it was difficult to be detached, let things slide; then the restraint he put upon himself was more brutal than a scene. Now by force of not saying what he thought, it was impossible to know what he thought, or feel what he thought. But if he said his mind, his phobia released, righted itself, shifted its centre, the situation changed, and his excitement was stupid for another thing obsessed him. And when they talked together, it was haltingly and with long silence, but if they met in love, silence too was overpowering.

He hated her. He wished she were with him and he could tell her this; but she would look at him, he would lose his words, drown in her. And if he said it, she would cry and cling to him, scold, then forgive him, tomorrow have forgotten; but she could not forget what she looked forward to. Her eyes looked forward but her life, her lives were in the past. When she looked back she would not see him nor his fellows. He was with the pack. Some nights, or if she were moved or in wine, he would howl through her. Some part of him would mingle with her, with them, in violent hysterical proximity. And if he never saw her again yet he would still be part of her, in ghastly intimacy meet his successors, his predecessors. All that was out of his control who could not forever withhold himself.

That was edifying he thought wryly; it explained everything and it was a good thing she was gone, but still he wished her with him. The truth was it was painful to think and if she were with him he could throw himself into his eyes, wait for her words like a dog for a bone, his senses quivering round it. And if she were too hot or too cold, concern would devastate him, he would suffer as she suffered, be able to think of nothing till she smiled. Her face was set and he was miserable, wondering had he or what made her unhappy, but if some tic made her lips move, he thought she would smile and smiled too, warm in a rush of happiness.

How had he become such part of another, so completely compensatory, feeling he must protect her from all impact. Was it her, or his own tranquillity he cherished, and if the latter, why not loneliness. But he could not go from her, must always drag her after him, be vulnerable through her and half his energy live like a wall about her. Her anger made him timid, her fears so strengthened him, he could measure his new strength in units of energy. And continually he whittled away the elements which obscured his febrile vibration to her and consciously he had flung away what stood in the way of such response. Now he vibrated perpetually, tapping the air, all currents puzzling him. His solidity was illusion. Like the squat crayfish he took stock of the world through quivering antennae, but under his carapace shook with emotion. That love which was so vague to him, intangible, omnipresent, had withdrawn itself; his life was purposeless, with no one to approve him. And when he thought of her, he saw no face before him, no limbs, but a painful yearning with Angela for its name wrapped him round, chilling his skin with bitterness.

It was growing dark, recalling him to himself. The faces round him grew still and white. A pale watery light from the sheet flooded the tent, and a throbbing pole of light turning upon itself pushed at it through the air. Greasy black, dry grey, chocolate sepia moved deliberately on the screen, found shape, took on life. That flicker of shadow on deeper shadow was a substitute for his thoughts, moving in him with strange shapes. Out of the screen, a face swam up to him, at first remote, small, its surface matt; coming closer, growing larger, the skin of a cheek immensely magnified into rough crevices of powder, the corners of the eye vast fields of pulp dribbling a heart-breaking revolting moisture. The eyes moved with effort in sticky sockets, the lips twitched painfully, impossibly, and a glycerine tear crept heavily down the cheek. The face swam nearer; the eyes grew more glassy, expressionless, drifting like clouds over him, sucking him into a white frozen lake of grief. Like a ghost the face grew larger till it passed through and beyond him, moving onward with blind eyes, groping to some light of which he could not be aware. He saw them come up to him, for a moment lie wonderingly on his own, impalpably vanish.

Outside a barrel organ played, there was a noise of swaying trees in the canvas roof and he was by a river. In pale morning small waves ran past him, their pale crests made a little clapping noise. It was Russia, tardy spring, the buds opening with effort. There was a shed, tables, and he thought perhaps there had just been a party. Yet while he took his ease, foreboding of riot chilled his teeth in fear and rage, and in the tortuous alleys of some river port, far far away, Bordeaux perhaps, a dark quivering mass fought and shouted; but louder were the shrill cries and moans of someone they were tearing. And a great noise of lamentation rang on the air, and after, silence. But the port was far, how could he know what happened in it and came to himself shuddering, thinking water, drops, that voice on what flood, oh god, 'the lifeless tongue did make a certain lamentable noise as though it still yet spake and both the banks in mourning wise made answer to the same!'

She was so far away but her voice throbbed through him carried by water, clapping dryly in his mind or hesitating rustling like the dry leaves autumn rubs together, and like the purring gaslight her voice rose shuddering into shrill dry laughter while they swarmed about her, pushing her bewildered from one gaping face to another, not knowing was it a game or why they hated her, or if she were happy to be so in dispute or fearful of some terrible immolation. But an orgasm of doubt kept her mind from terror, only her voice, uncontrollable, rose quivering in his mind, leaping and falling, tearing his nerves, filling him with a mad longing to go at once to her, tear, fight, struggle to her, fall on her, blanket her shrieks. Blinded, his heart pounding, he came to himself again, depressed and impotent, his rage for activity sour inside him. Some wild melody had for a moment torn all his nerves, left him quivering. Her head and harp...

Dreams, the cone, its fearful apex plunging into starry cold, that velvet and intense black hole round which, beneath the world, the milky way flows like a rushing stream.

Anxious! And the hotel. Quickly he left the tent, pushing through darkness in a pillar of cloud, but walking had sought refuge, was in a door, flying in darkness, from someone, with difficulty, up stairs. His heart was pounding and like a blow an immense oval filled with light took his breath. Round him tier on tier of faces, packed oranges, shifting uneasily in the dry mutter which like rubbing chitin oozed from them. In the roof's semi-dark four lamps descended, deliberate insects, hovering with beams which burst with a glare of sunlight on white sand over the tiny square where two small shadows rushed at each other in a sickening impact of blows. He was feinting, plunging, shuddering at each blow, dancing on his seat, his suppressed cries and excitement that found no outlet a fever. Deceived, flat, the fight ended, the light waned... he was in the street under the pouring noise. The air glowed pink and rose with light that came from paper lanterns. On a platform, boys in flannels, girls in short white skirts, drilled, swung in parallel bars, leapt over each other under the whirling chairs, which snatched at each other, turning on themselves. It dragged his eyes, a monstrous game was being played with him and however he snapped, it must flash tantalising past. Before him lay the street, so tight his heart sank, feeling he could never push into it, but it opened to him, drawing him softly, packing itself comfortingly, dragging and pushing, and releasing him staggering into the open space at the end.

The relief of empty square, night, quiet, was a sudden loosening of oppressive bands. A quite unreasonable, somehow infantile elation half frightened him; he was growing smaller, tighter, and so was his face. He was so full not even Angela could hurt him. What could so have worried him? The prospect of innumerable bored hours, the sleepless nights, the long colloquies when no strange breath drugged him, no soft belly held his hand. Yet all had been his and another had taken them. Taken what, he asked himself... all was so remote. With joy his brain rose free from all that pain. He'd kept the grove, the golden bough, in a thousand hazards and through his own despair, till that too heavy burden, once so light, in monstrous isolation filled his mind. That grew at length too much, till one day, absent, worn, and wanting to be worn, some other snatched a bough, that earnest of her being. Now she must seek that charm; and turns from him, not needing him. So he died.

But agonising thought, before all thought went, that new priest would care more for it, nay make it his delight. Had he himself been other, that too had been his paradise. How bravely the tree trembles over his fading eyes, how could it so oppress him. He cannot remember his pangs nor in a moment his joys. The tree waves wanton shimmering, distant and dancing light. That only is everlasting, his own life trivial. Yet he revolted. All is fading.

He turned his mind resolutely away. When he touched the edge of his preoccupations, his elation went thin, about to vanish. That frightened him. He must not let it go and find himself intensely alone with his obsession. He should hurry back to the hotel, change, eat dinner, go out again, but where he did not know. The evening was falling rapidly together. So little remained and all so tightly packed, he must cut through it with immense arm wavings, lungings, heavings.

Monica was waiting in his room. He said still here, and began to change quickly, careless of her gloom. When he turned to go, he said now stop it, I cant be bothered. To his astonishment she smiled, and they went down to dinner. In the corridor she tried to kiss him but he pushed her away, O come on!

One side of the restaurant was a steamy plate glass window, but through the glaucous tiles of the walls dolphins bounced in choppy blue waves and eels nosed among hovering starfish. Ferns sprouted in brass pots, from brass pots under the ceiling ferns crawled into the air. The electric fan turned on itself, shivering like a jellyfish, its streamers waving into the room, the haze of breath. The white cloths, red shades, made the air limpid and yet charged, himself, the room, deep in waving water. Sometimes a white shirt swam to the surface of the immense brass pot as for a breath. He enjoyed his long dinner. Monica fidgeted. He said: Now well go to the aquarium. Then we can have our fun.

155

She looked gratefully at him.

Gaily they pushed into the crowd, the same crowd that gliding, eddied in the same places, rushed or loitered in the same places, a dense mass moving like a dark river on which in opposite direction moved other faces, bright, or in the shadow of hats, teeth suddenly, some deep orbit, wild mustaches: and always the blank pink ovals, content to be among so many, the burden of themselves lifted by themselves. The pounding noise made the air swirl, the whirling lights filled the pulsing air, poured over the crowd, filled it with vitality.

From time to time Monica would push up to him, murmuring you do love me, dont you, and he pushed roughly back, saying yes, or no, or do shut up. But both were happy that the air was no longer charged, and his gaiety was an armour through which her longings could not pierce. Now spongy and humid dark buoyed them up. Gaping unwinking fish nosed at them through square green portholes, glided to earth like birds, like birds swam up through yellow weeds or settled pecking into the fine sand like a flight of starlings; flat fish undulated rapidly across the tank like galloping horses, their eyes starting, their bellies rasing the earth, or flurried in the cascade of bubbles which spluttering into the tank rose again to run in clots of quicksilver on the waters surface.

Some click of stone struck his middle ear; some other fish. Her cries came to him upon the water, she gaped bewildered in the hard ways his jealousy had circumscribed. Her watery world was wide. His heart leapt yearning after her. She swam from him through the cold sea, fluttering tight and small, her mind a blank but lured to a treacherous luminous point, or rose and sank to a vibration, not sensed by him. Undine...yet she had come to him. Transfuse me...give me a soul. How, why? Now he would not see the cheeks flush with blood again, the eyes soften, the breast rise, and his own soul was flying from him inside her, she unwitting; yet he must find her again where like a box, remotely hid she held his heart, a 'vanishing wife'. But it could not be himself had sent her off and there had been no compact. No compact, true, nothing was said, yet drifting to land, had he not pulled a twig, had it not cried out warning him, and when as though despite himself he plucked another, had she not come from the river.

She was black but comely, intimidating him, the Ishmael of his tribe. But since she loved him, seemed less comely in his eyes, and he embellished by her love, her better. Sometimes he loved her, loving him; for that too he hated her. She had endowed him with houses clearings slaves, on one condition which repetition made most burdensome. How long he had rebelled, though once such love went with it. Later he thought, why fish-heads, and why nine, and what past did they light, and to what future point. What new compulsion on the morrow. Best end it.

That fear held him and his doubt grew stronger. On eight days he said No! caught back the slave, himself cut off the heads, took them in to her unsmiling. The ninth boy was too quick, he saw him wing into the house, a whole fish in his hand, too quick to stop. While he gapes the jungle walks in his clearing, palms wave in his thatch, pigs root in his plantations.

Alone again, he asks himself when that first doubt grew, and why he had not plucked that weed, foreboding told him must take root in his weed fed mind which chokes in yearning for her. He dreams, is back where he started, a child again and weak. No years have intervened.

A milky moon of glass gave a virulent daylight of eclipse and white faces swam past them, the eyes dark sockets, solemn as the sea horses falling indolently through the water, their heads low hung in meditation, or else erect on a curled tail they drifted through water, the fin twirling busily like a propeller, the ears turning like a winged cap of Mercury, till a twig or mate gave hold to the anchoring tail. They clung to each other, their beady eyes looking a knowing content, their progress through the water grave, their dense agglomerations rising and falling on a contented corporate swell. That stilled the tumult which had begun to rise in him at thought of her; and a sparkle of gaiety replaced it before the next tank, where transparent shining, among bright reeds outlined in glittering bubbles bright upon the dark background, hung from invisible wires the equilateral triangles of fish pulled iridescent through the water. They were so still, only a glowing eye and dark vertical band opaque in the charmed area; their bull-like profiles hieratic and unmoved. Yet next them a dense clot of anemones with deliberate swaying tentacles like a monstrous picture disquieted him, their brick reds, rotting whites and porous yellows transporting him to a lunar vegetation where his mind crawled and stumbled through a carnivorous forest.

Monica was tugging at his sleeve. They moved on to where against dark rock the green was almost blue. In apoplectic scarlet, bristling appendages like Japanes warriors, four crayfish sat deep in holes, but for a long way on either side their heads stretched the slow antennae, criss-crossing like the lances of Uccello. Only, near the mouth, a small appendage shuddered incessantly. That betrayed them, their carapaces solid, but within all was uncontrollable tremor. And two tiny claws near the mouth moved over and over each other, perpetually cleaning something. Like a once seen mantis which for hours, for unendurable days, drew its slatted antennae through its microscopic giraffes jaws, its filmy skirts puffing out from the tiny waist. Like Angela, feeling her hair, or plucking her lips or washing; her daydreams a perpetual preparation of cleaning as was her awakening and her bedgoing. A crowd hemmed him in, he could not breathe; when he looked round, Monica had gone. He saw a curtain and she was behind it. Threads of gut hung in water, glittering parachutes, falling arc lamps. Transparent the gut glowed, carrying dull stars in crinkled invisible streamers which slowly changed their length, the creature rising, falling, deliberate and all but water. It had a will, it shone with its own light.

Next, diaphanous, floated, an elliptical ball, along whose seams flickered an unending run of rainbow light, blue, green, yellow, red, like his thoughts, hate, fear, yearning and what else he wondered, seeing them run effortlessly into each other.

In the last jar a curled end of thick transparent tape, flapped rainbow light along its oblong edges, like running fire flung from theatre façades to dazzle all the sky. What gave that light? The parachute alone lived round a misty spot, entrails perhaps and batteries, but these rest? They were water; the rapid vibration and flash of cilia marked their bounds, made their identity; the unbodied restless run of fire trembled broke trembled, like the ceaseless tremor of the crayfishs appendages. The alcove grew too hot, they went again into the sombre body of the hall, and there was another tank.

At first they saw nothing, then hard against a rock the octopus, soft speckled with eel-like arms, bronze coins of suckers. While they watched, a spiracle large as a sixpence opened, then shut, its fine edges blowing open and shut, each arm, its body, twitching, moving, as if the whole creature meant to move. Nothing happened, the hurried movement of the spiracle accelerated, the tentacles shuddered more quickly, the skin twitched everywhere, a dark bead-eye peered for a moment, and while they looked, a fish fell through the tank and like a sudden cloud a squid rose into the water, its arms dragging gracefully after it. There was a long Oh-h from the people round him and a sudden crush to see more of the thing, which heaped now upon itself in a corner of the tank like a rock, suffused its transparent skin with rushing purple shadows, its beak sawing into the rigid fish.

As in the music-hall: the back cloth ripples shimmering purple and gold, dark reeds which catch the glittering bubbles, the wings dark glittering too. And the transparent air is glassy. While in that icy cage, fixed for an eternity, of no time and for ever, red faces gape, soundless as a fish. Yet the air vibrates. The pianist's notes clash like wood, the bowels yearn to the yearning cello, through the wide mouth and stake-like teeth a voice swells like a bubble and the solicitation of the harpist draws out, scatters, a cascade of air, a fountain bubbling and complaining. The sounds vibrate and cut each other, the colours merge into and take from each other, are fluid and separate, and the set is immutable for eternity. In the long spiral of time only the onlooker changes and must change. And because he changed, their contact with him inoculated them with the first germs of change, they too corrupted. And she whom he desired, who was eternal too, crumbled in contact with him, and because of him betrayed him at all points.

He was wedged by the crowd, and tight within it; but an insistent hand which he had tried to ignore was on his arm. He turned, saw Angela. Suddenly that anguish which all day had vibrated in him fell away, leaving him solid, as though she poured herself, quicksilver, into all his veins. He began to breathe again, his chest that had been tight, expanded, his blood flowed easily. And his anguish? He could not remember it. She smiled with parted lips and the wide luminous eyes looked at him with pleasure. He had come out of a nightmare, her proximity comforted him, his demons had left him, gone back into her, the mask of her face hiding the ravage they made in her. How could he know what she felt? But he must nöt enquire and if she left him again, again the pack would spill out over him. He was safer by her side and a sudden apprehension that she might go frightened him. Wondering, he looked into her face, but saw nothing. Some act of God had stormed mountains into valleys, piled seas on mountains. She had come. Now all was changed and his way lost in her. How could he know her again? Yet he watched her face with blind eager faith and because she smiled was happy. And when she put out her hand, saying darling, his heart turned over and he followed her to a corner where she threw her arms round him, sighing deeply, pressing her lips to his own. His every question faded, yet he said, but what. Were you unhappy?

No, not unhappy!

But why — tell me — talk to me — what are you doing here?

I dont know. I thought I would come in.

Have you been to the hotel.

No!

I cant understand. How can you stand there? Is all my suffering nothing to you?

Have you suffered?

He looked at her, his lips trembling.

Had he suffered? Too much! his heart said, pounding. But what is it? Why are you here? Dont you love me?

Yes, I love you!

But how — how could you — and where have you been?

I dont know. He wanted me!

But I wanted you.

Yes, I know.

I suppose he was new.

I suppose so.

The eyes glimmered, the eyeballs darted to the side of her head.

And why leave him now? Isnt he suffering?

I dont know.

He shook her roughly. What is it? Are you ill?

No, not ill.

Angela, darling, what is it?

Nothing.

Monica had come up to them with a rush, babbling, but she turned away coldly. I dont like women.

But its Monica, he said.

I know.

Monica was trembling, wringing her hands beseechingly, but Angela went out of the tent and they followed her. It was she he had seen. She had avoided him. But her treachery, which at another moment might have hurt him, seemed justified, the subject now for explanation; he was glad, for later she would talk, tell him she loved him, explain. Anxiously he followed her, and once she turned as though encouragingly, moving rapidly through the crowd. Her voice was still in his ears, now it fled on the swift current, dragging his entrails. She had been torn, was being torn. He saw her swim rapidly from him, seeking some charm for her hurt, and Monica followed in distress, seeing both fly from her. He came up with her in a stuffy bare bar, sat at her marble table. She looked furiously at him, her head on her hands, her eyes looking sideways, and started when Monica came, then for a long time there was silence. Suddenly she turned to him. What are you doing with that woman?

What do you mean? How dare you?

She got up to go, but he pushed her back. Sit down, you cant go again.

Monica looked hurt, puzzled. Do you really hate me, Angela?

But there was no reply; the pale eyes flashed equivocal.

Too disgusting. I leave you for a moment and youre with that woman.

O! said both in revolt.

I cant think why I came back.

Angela! said Monica, crying, and went out of the café. O now Ive hurt her. I have hurt her, she said in distress. Do fetch her back.

He made no move. Yes! youve hurt her. What does it matter? She wont mind tomorrow and youll have forgotten.

But she rose as though to fetch her.

O do sit down.

She turned smiling to him. Come and sit here.

He sat by her. Turned towards him, a glass in one hand, minutely she looked into his face, his eyes. What did she see? Nothing had changed him. She was not lost in him. He seemed older, tired. Did I hurt you, she asked, hopefully.

He smiled. Yes!

Large tears were forming in her eyes. Like a ghost her face grew larger, reaching towards him, drifting wonderingly through his own. His own eyes filled and he said: Come out!

He held her arm tightly. She was his world, cold to his fingers. She began to tremble. He hated her for it. There was too much he did not know. But he thought too it might be because she was with him, was mollified and held her tighter. O if she shuddered because she was with him, then all was well. Darling, dont be miserable, really its all right! She smiled at him. Some moments are too painful, he told himself, and the thought took the edge off his pain. But what was she thinking? Neither thinking nor feeling. She was blank to him, a flint-hard surface nothing could scratch.

Then he could mean nothing to her. That depressed him. How ask himself was she bad or good, for her, for himself? That was not the point. So vague all was. She walked on the walls, her eyes frightened, her face veiled, yet she could assure him of himself. He loved her and his life was full. He hated her and his life was full, but between those poles life was arid for either; they hung upon each other, destroying, thwarting. Better that than lose her, she was so much part of him. But what inexplicable desire, startling, surprising, gratifying him, threw her suddenly in his arms, crushing him, tears in her flying eyes, her voice broken, as though she loved him, more, needed him, forcing the old gesture, as though they were part of each other. Later she would veil herself, recede. She told him he loved her and he believed it. But

160

instinctively he knew he was hallucinated, his only excuse that he had for a moment held her, indued her with his love, his lusts, like so many.

Yet he could not think she had not come back to him, though at any moment she might go. Im so glad youre back, are you glad youre back, he wanted to say but said nothing. What could she say but Yes!

It was not her words, but that was all he had to believe in. What had he ever had? His uncertainty and even his resentment he had no right to, was bewildered by them. She had imposed him on herself and it was important to him to feel necessary to her. Illusion. Yet she was with him, but for how long, and why? She might leave him soon. That was most strange, most inexplicable. Had he seemed as far from her as she from him, that morning, when he felt no converging roads could ever in the wide world bring them together again? And what vow could he tear from her deepest heart to make her stay? And after, her face would turn cold, then he would urge her to go, and she would go or stay, unmask or grow harder. He stopped thinking. She knew what currents she must sink or rise into. But it comforted him that his heart, fluttering, hiding, would always follow, watch. And if she saw it she would be touched or irritated. Madness not to be able to count on her. What was she and from what childhood did she come to him, and what did she bring?

Impulses, fears, preoccupations, anxieties, what had made inevitable their collision and what now forced them away? By distant tortuous ways he had come to meet her and he thought she to meet him. He held her, but they could not meet again.

Yes, he held her and from time to time she turned gratefully to him, but he knew there was a wall between them.

Yet she trembled, perhaps had trembled yesterday, held by another. But that thought did not bring her nearer. There were still walls. Something happened inside her, her lime salt reserve was high or low, her walls were up or down; she would not share with him if they dictated it. Sometimes a sponge is hard, sometimes is soft, always impenetrable. Could he percolate into her and the woman who held his heart, where was she?

He made an effort and came out of that watery waste in which he tracked her, caught her to him. One must be simple. There was a giant racer and he led her to it. Lets try this. But she shuddered away, ah no! While they stood, Monica, her face flushed, her hair flying and her hat in her hand, a man at her side, was coming out.

O Angela! Its too marvellous. Do come on, it is so thrilling. Her excitement was contagious, and brightened him but Angela shuddered. I couldnt. O I cant. Yet each supporting an arm they led her falteringly to the car. Her lips against his face, her eyes shut, she waited for each vertiginous swoop, her breath so caught he thought he held her heart. Some warmth from her made him feel she came back to him. On his other side Monica yelled with delight, with terror, her fingers pressing into his knee, while round them people howled, and on the crest from which the rails plunged vertically into darkness, shudderingly gasped.

Light streaked far below and into the distance. He saw the dark heath, its glittering lights, the tent in which for a moment she had come to him and his heart had broken. Yet he held her, yet she was real. That was what he could not convince himself of. Madness. He had seen her torn, her pale singing head upon the river. How long he had sought her and still did, yet he knew he would not find her. A woman lives in the house, sits opposite you at meals or sews, is sweet or cross, pale sometimes; in the dark her hair crackles under the comb and sometimes the silk shift crackles with blue sparks. She has her thoughts: they take her browsing through the night. You ask yourself why she stays, wonder why she does not go, then she is with another. All grows dark.

The car came to a stand, they staggered with wavering knees into a bar, but Angela scowled at them and while they drank her eyes shifted under the frowning eyebrows. After a time she said to Monica, I thought youd gone.

Her escort rose, threatening. I wont have Monica spoken to that way; and Dick rose angrily too, as though it were expected of him, but Angela said, O sit down, do lets drink something. And Monica too said to her escort, do shut up, whats it got to do with you?

The room grew dirtier, smokier, the lights more pallid. He was looking intently at Angelas face which now was drawn and tired like that of a cherished sickly child. She had been lost. He saw her hurrying through a cold, sun-filled square, naked under the thin dress, or in lamplit night, alone but with her demons; her frock torn open, rain beating the white skin, the darkness at her core forcing the eye down in wretched violence. Behind her face the deep holes in her skull bored into other holes in other skulls, in yearning apprehension, her very carriage apprehensive. Had she been a stranger to him he must have looked after her in painful wonder at that frantic haste which feared everything. What death and corruption had been her earliest food to make her so passionate for life, her stars impelling her through zones of death; the war or water, aeroplanes or motors, killed those she loved. So her love too was now a death, the sacred ties a deliquescence. That passion which now but in seeming filled her, in another must have forced deep significance and solemn warning upon each stone. Those stones were sacred. Yet that street saw her with another and with others and no stone rose in witness against her, she who was, was not a stone. They were the witness of her triumph. She brought her trembling victims to the stench of earlier sacrifices, her bemused mind already ranging new fields for other conquests. And the man hurried too, bewildered, seeming to long to loiter, but part of her mysterious greed.

That picture was eternal. He saw her projected upon innumerable sunlit squares, lamplit shining streets, hurrying, seeking, frantic. Behind, protesting, a man or himself. Yet she had left that frame, come back to him. Yet she would go from him. Now she was silent with tired angry eyes.

They drank in silence. After a time the tiredness faded from her face, the mouth smiled, the cheeks grew full, the chin plump and the eyes clear. She put her hand out and generously pressed his own. That was heartrending, but he was glad too. A clock struck midnight and the street, when they went out, was empty; the polished road shining under the lamps, reflecting even the starlight which, like a cloud of sulphur butterflies, had settled upon the sand, throbbing and sucking up the moisture left by a receding tide. By the light of flares men in shirt-sleeves were taking down booths, the loosened canvas flapping loudly in the night wind, dust and paper swirling.

In air they were suddenly drunk and Angela began to run, bounding like a child, like a herd, as light as air and then heavy, he following. She put her arms round him and it was a woman, alive, laughing, hanging to him, kissing him warmly, wanting to climb. He felt she soared, was rising into the air and clung to her, holding her back. But again she ran from him, touching the walls, the door handles, as she went, peering into windows, hiding in shadow, coming into light, like the changing light and darkness of a tree, plucking at his hand to pull him after her, and he followed willingly, happy to be wanted, wishing to have her to himself.

They were in the open where the marquees had stood. Their dark skeletons were black on the sky. Men in the light of flares bent over stacks of canvas. The heath was waste, the sky empty, lowering. Vaguely he dreamed of an immense luminous face upon his own, growing larger against the sky. Before he could stop her she was swarming up a pole. He pulled her roughly down and she clung to him, her face near his own, growing nearer till it was utterly on his own.

Against his will he put up his lips to her.

The others had come up, Monica silent and furious, and the change from her late meekness surprised him. The man was green, his eyes sunk, his jaws working, his whole being staggering as though about to rend itself, and insolently he waved his arms in a futile gesture. He remembered the snake woman and led them to her. Her china eyes were glazed, she rocked on her feet, the snake was heavily round her neck, the battered features sagged in an unwilling smile. She was surprised to see him and for a long time could not understand what he said, repeating foolishly, eh, cocky? But when Angela pulled at the snake begging to handle it, the film flickered from her eyes; she suddenly woke, gave its nose a rapid lick, and asking them to wait, disappeared, leaving Angela with the snake round her neck. Its body hung solid; occasionally the eyes blinked, the head reared a little or swam from her, its restless tongue slipping in and out. She still clung to it in the taxi and despite their remonstrances would not be parted from it. From time to time its owner caressed its head in the warm triangle of her closing palm.

The dim, low room in which they later found themselves was like other low rooms. White tiles, a scarlet bench round the wall, a cash desk and a woman like a dummy behind it, writing minute figures on a large block. After a while there was a waiter who looked at them, started a little when he saw the snake, went away. They sat against the wall and Angela was by his side. In his peace he had half forgotten she was with him. The snake hung round her neck and she could not keep her hands from it till its owner in sudden jealousy took it from her. The waiter came back, hesitated, came nearer, took their order, went away again.

A negro with a gaudy scarf round his loins came into the room. He was bronze in the light and an enormous smile shone in the cropped head, everted lips, triangular teeth. He sat with them and his hand caressed the snakes jaws, and innocent and contented he asked them for brandied cherries. Dicks half-smoked cigarette dropped from his fingers. He bent to pick it up, but she stopped him, its dirty. Yet it obsessed him and furtively he kicked it nearer. But she placed her foot on it, too disgusting, how can you?

That was too much. He was suddenly kneeling on the floor, pushing her shoe aside, but her feet fought with him, and when he had forced her legs the lamentable stub of frayed tobacco brought him to his senses. How could he, he wondered. It seemed disgusting to her he should want it again after the filthy floor. Yesterday he would have thought so himself. But he still regretted it and could not believe she had destroyed it. That part of his mind which held the immortality of love, held the immortality of cigarette ends.

He got out from under the table, sat erect again, tearing himself painfully from the comfort of her skirts.

The room was beginning to fill, his companions stared vaguely into the room; Monicas escort grimaced crossly at the negro; the snakewomans nose hung over her glass.

The light faded. A cold, smoky smell invaded the room. Angela felt something hard against her hand and shrieked. It was the snake. A scarlet lime was shot through the room and small blue lights flashed off the heads of negroes massed upon the platform. In one movement all put coruscating tubes to their monstrous lips. He felt their gold teeth must be flashing too. A loud bray of music began to paw them, the limes revolved rapidly, plum, orange, green, blue, and small brilliant lights continued to buzz off the heads, eyeballs and instruments like a swarm of bluebottles around a dunghill.

The room was suddenly full. They twirled in couples over the floor, the girls fat, trustful, in spectacles, busily chewing; their legs twitching, buttocks rocking on a fulcrum, progressing minutely round the floor. His whole face was absorbing light, a plate glass window. The music rocked faster, sleepier, the dancing couples hurried; and when some polished surface caught the limes, small lights flew off; so that the room glimmered and winked and the mirrors round the wall were full of a myriad fluttering insects dancing round pale faces, from which sombre eyes gloomed under masses of pale hair, bursting like the aloe. And the music rocked through the room and strong male voices rolled upon it as on a deep comforting flood, uplifting his heart. They were solid, but the white faces were ill, life weighed too heavily on them, they peered furtively at it.

The music ended, the light was white again, there was a hurried shuffling of chairs and the room was suddenly too full. And through it all the cold smell of smoke. All five were in a trance, the bottles empty.

The lights went dark again and a scarlet lime beat full on the platform. Suddenly there was a small negro in dinnerjacket, top hat, half bent on himself, frantically dancing a sort of clog dance, his coat-tails flying, his heels jigging, his hands waving, teeth flashing, face wide open in a spasmodic grin. The music hurried, his tic was more violent. With anguish they waited for exhaustion to stop him, but his body bending nearer the ground, leaping high, falling on one foot, then on the other, jigging, jerking he went on, till in a sympathetic frenzy the audience rose to its feet, violently clapping. That suddenly cut his energy; he staggered off. In his place stood a girl. A pearl glowed in her ear like a moon. Such legs! And her face was Cleopatras in the British Museum. Her skin was green-yellow, an unripe and downy peach, and her voice rose so sour, so sweet, he could not bear it. She was looking for a lamb, and her voice, bubbling, moaning, complaining, shuddered and died tremulously murmuring, a child sobbing itself asleep. And again her voice rose mournful, swaying like the snake: I couldnt hear nobody pray, he gnashed his teeth, with my saviour by my side, his heart grew stronger, I couldnt hear nobody pray. He saw Babylon in a great sheet of fire, half the sky cut by lightning; terraces, frantic princes and their concubines in too heavy jewelled gowns, chariots galloping into the yawning earth.

Her negroes were behind her like a wall, they swayed on bent knees, jigging up and down with an immense brooding composure, thrown back upon themselves, a sombre cloud round each bulging forehead. The stage was full of them, infinitely various, different races almost; their dead white and ebony went through every shade of green and indigo and certain eyes gleamed like green enamel in obsidian masks; so many sizes, shapes, weights could not be human, must be toys, the pekinese and mastiff, marmoset and great ape, dolls bottle and carboy. The contrast of large and small was infinitely touching and an enormous woman had the scarlet, spongy lips and receding profile of a carp. She took her wig off and it was a man; and all the time they fretillated like fish with fierce epileptic vitality and the room filled with an intense, disheartening smell.

Some ritual dance. In a clearing, bird-large moths knock out the torches. Idols squat under an immense vertical moon. Land crabs rustle in the grass. What longing filled her face, dilated her eyes, parted her lips, suspended her breath. Her face was swimming out into the night, upon the sky, seeking some answer. He could not help her. He did not know what she looked for, what new thing she would bring back. It would mean much to her. It would shut him out and afterwards she would forget it and he unhappily be too far to come back. He turned from her with disgust. The snake was still and the woman who nursed it silent. Monica and her friend were rubbing knees. The room was a haze of smoke, the faces white, drawn. The place was dark again but a radiance came from table cloths and faces. A drum began to beat, first deliberate, then fast. It was their own pulses. It made the heart beat stronger. A red lime floated on the air and on the stage a girl began to turn slowly while her belly moved with a continuous circular motion, then flapped convulsively to a high braying reed which cut the air, her face hanging remote and solicitous over it. The snake had put its head out, swaying to and fro, peering at one and another, not understanding.

More girls came on the stage. They were pink, smiling in straw hats, white shoes and white suits. They shuffled in a circle, their hands hovering above each others buttocks, their feet rasping in sand with a monotonous, satisfying sound, like pushing an immense weight up a hill. And when suddenly the room was in darkness, their clothes were luminous, startling; the boots, shoes, combinations, disembodied: shuffling with a slow, maddening rhythm.

Monicas man stood up, swaying, green; yelled and was among them, shuffling with them, his hands fluttering, his face floating, his senses swaying in their emanations and the room rose to its feet shouting encouragement at him, but the spell was broken and Monica walked quietly down the room and dragged him back to his seat.

His own peace grew deeper, stupefying. The air was heavy, warm, and he could not breathe. He went out of the room into the lavabos. He came out and Angela stood there trembling.

I thought you had gone.

Darling, how could I?

Her face was on his own, the mouth twisted. You wont leave me.

But of course not.

Dick, dont leave me.

It was fresh in the anteroom among the glazed tiles. An old woman sat over a plate of brass coins, engrossed in her knitting. Through the door he saw the long room in darkness and curling smoke billowing in the fluffy rope of the lime. People passed continually by them, emerging women holding lip sticks, pausing at the glass, going away.

The cistern gurgled. He thought they had never been so alone. She had left him; she had come back. He shook her and she clung to him. What do you want with me?

I love you. I cant live without you.

And yesterday?

She looked at him mournfully, reproachfully. I loved you too.

How can you be so stupid?

But I did!

What do you mean, you could not.

Do understand. He wanted me. I had to. Her head hung in despair. Dont leave me, even if you cant love me. I wouldnt you.

I dont understand you, he said, but his mind saw her hurrying through a sunlit square, her eyes glazed, yet darting; her fingers holding, forgetting. I dont know what you want! he said then in deep depression.

No, but I came back.

Yes, he got sick of you.

No, she said violently, and for the first time with passion.

Else you wouldnt be here.

Why not, I left you for him.

Not for long. Not really. You would have liked to.

Why do you hurt me so?

How could you go so wantonly, I hate you.

O you cant.

Yes.

She turned away in despair, but came back. Dont send me away.

Yes, Im bored. Its a rotten situation. You made it yourself too. There was no need to go.

But I told you he wanted me.

I cant believe you, you wanted him, or you were afraid someone else might. Frightful to think you cant let one get by you. Me too you followed, when I fled from you.

I dont know; it is all over; really it is.

How can it be? For you yes, but never for me. And feverishly he asked: What did he have I couldnt give you?

He wanted me, she said, with sombre pride.

Did I hate you then, he asked, his shamed eyes watering, feeling that somewhere perhaps, hidden in himself, sensed only by her, that hatred lay. He would have promised anything rather than go on talking, wanted to hurt, frighten her. And she was nearer to him when he held her off. You hurt me; you go away. Why should I go on being hurt?

But I love you.

Its been awful.

I know. I had to come back. I have too. She was crying.

That hardened him. But where is he? What have you done with him? He was afraid she might tell him who it was.

That man was suddenly too important, he filled the room. He sat in a train, a hotel room, and Angela was with him. They moved to and fro in it with small gestures and his own part in her was now part of that other. Some part of himself now lived anonymously, anywhere, even his bastards were not his own. How could he know what part of him she had given away, or everything or nothing! Why not be furious when somewhere it is still indecent to eat in public. Or perhaps that man too, like himself, would not listen to her, had vainly tried to hold back the pack. And if they met, what could they pretend to ignore when every gesture or smile must betray each to the other. For each his new relation must be ghastly, but she was glad men thought of her in the far quarters of the globe. Or if indeed sometime he would not care, then all was worse.

She said, I dont know where he is. I came away. Hes gone on.

Yes, and at any moment, hell come back, take you away again.

O no! she said sadly. I couldnt.

And anywhere at any moment I may hear him say, Yes, she bored me with her love or 'her breasts'.

Dont, dont go on!

I hate you, he said sadly.

Dont, dont, she was clutching at him, stroking his arm wildly. I shall kill myself.

Yes, kill yourself.

She did not seem to hear him, but in a moment her eyes widened, her mouth fell open in horror. Kill myself, she said as though he had said it. Oh, I couldnt. She was silent, her mouth beginning to work suddenly. Do say something to me. Do say its all right. If you look at me so I shall feel I have to go again, find some assurance. But I know you want me, that you do love me. You do, dont you?

She might be right. Certainly her need for assurance put assurance into his mind to give back to her. And to himself it was proof. How strange she should feel she needed as a proof that assurance which she had given him, and which would be given back to her. He did not want her, but he could not say it. But she knew what she wanted, increasing herself through him, a transformer, getting back to herself. And her mind which simulated doubt was clear.

What am I to do with you. His head too was clearing, his anguish seemed false to him. How could he not believe her? But tomorrow all could so easily happen again. Women still went in and out, turning heavy eyes on them. He saw themselves as they must seem, pale, with deep eyes vibrating to each other, solid-seeming.

I was frantic. When I got away there was only you in my head. You will think that proves I wanted to go, but I was too miserable to stay away. I thought you were miserable. But I was afraid too, felt guilty, didnt know what to do. It seemed easier to go on going away. I couldnt face you. How could I? It seemed so impossible to ask you to forgive me. And there seemed nothing to forgive.

He thought he too would have behaved so; it was true there was nothing to forgive. Nothing had happened.

He believed her. How could he do anything else? What he wanted to be sure of was that she would not go again. But how to make sure of that?

There was still time for him to turn away. Then she would be in despair, unhappy resigned or furious: look like death, talk of suicide, till after a last burst of anger her letters died away, plaintively shuddering. A year, and she would have forgotten him. Rather than face that oblivion he would comfort her, grow more deeply still into her, give her time to find herself, and tranquil again turn to some new figure which should be all he had once seemed to her. He was only postponing it. He saw her suddenly, burnt terra cotta, her cheeks flushed, bending, a garden figure of a satyr at her back. She bent blindly; not happy nor unhappy, compelled by an imperious need, all her being absorbed.

Not happy nor unhappy. What had he to do with that blind force? It did not concern him and he had no part in it and his passion of jealousy was for a lust that did not include him. His rancour dropped.

Yet it always seemed new to her. Yet it still seemed to her the road must end joyfully as it began. She walked so many roads. How could she still be unaware that darkness was inevitably part of distance, the road narrowing, grown precipitous, the shadows falling, age too. She would start on her road with the same passion, knowing of course, but oblivious, that each new effort made the chain she dragged longer, heavier. And yet there was a chance another might take her chain, and yet she might find grace.

Why did he resent her sunward turning that was natural in any other creature. So many suns and one for each, yet which was false among the true. The moth might be in error yet paid for its conclusions. But Angela, flapping blindly round her sun, had lamentably involved him, and that he could not forgive. Yet armies had followed a girl and humanity enlisted under the banner of the telephone directory. His problem too would always be the same. Another man, hated, feared; would he stay in or get out. He would get out, his fear stronger than his hatred. His fear of what? Not of the man. Of the woman, then. Yes, and that was fear of himself. Go before she told him she respected him, was used to him; the proof, familiarity had made her dry, but another could make that flute note flash open, shut. Then what — nothing; but a conviction of impotence that would poison his life for a long time.

All that was too much of a weight he felt, and threw it off, straightening his back. She straightened too, smiling innocently, a full beam of trusting understanding vibrating to him. You wont leave me, she said then.

No, of course not.

Her face fell sombre again. The ordeal she had set herself was over and she could relax.

Monica was standing by them, furious. How much longer are we to wait for you? If you think it amusing — and your beastly snake woman drunk as can be. And how dare you tell me Angela had left you.

What has it to do with you anyway, and why are you so furious? Are you so poor your first thought is to defend yourself? And why do you shout as though I meant to criticise you, he half-shouted, following Angela back into the room, and even that short distance she walked feverishly with staccato steps, swaying.

The room was dark. A haze which held suspended tables, guests, lights. They came out of the white light of their conversation into the heavy vault-like smell of the room. Nothing had moved. The woman had her nose in the glass, her snake swaying from side to side, and the negro sat by her, looking fearfully at it, his own snake-teeth shining. When they sat down he looked happily at them and when he made a gesture the inside of his hand was crumpled pink, repulsive, the outside indigo and horny. It was strange there were now no women in the place, and while they sat they found themselves little by little surrounded by monstrous boys who quarrelled, fought, dabbed at each other with futile paws. Some were fat and pale, others darkly tragic, and they asked for brandied cherries appealingly, snuffling like the coati in the Small Cat House. One wore a toga, another sang a street song in a rich contralto, his blanket slipping from his shoulders, then made a collection. The negro seemed only half there, simple, his voice lost in his clicking, tied tongue. He was smiling to himself and with a look of false bewilderment held a paper for her to read to him. Halting often to ask if he understood her, she read to the negro from the wide black bordered sheet that smelt cold and smoky too.

†M

THE PRINCE KODJO
TOVALOU HOUENOU

Barrister at Law, President of the United League for the Defence of the Black Race; his brothers and sisters, his family and allied families, regret to inform you of the cruel loss sustained by them in the death of

His Royal Highness the King
(JOSEPH) TOVALOU PADONOU
AZANMODO HOUENOU

of the first royal dynasty of Dahomey, scion of the houses of Allada, Zado, Ouéme, Djigbe; Head of the family Houénou, Chevalier of the Legion of Honour, Member of the Order of the Black Star of Benin, The Order of Agricultural Merit, The Order of Cambodia;

Their Head, and father, grandfather, brother, cousin, uncle, nephew, father-in-law and deceased friend, at Ouidah the 1st of December in his 70th year and furnished with the sacraments of the Catholic Church.

And pray you to assist at the funeral ceremonies to take place on Monday, December 21st, at 7 o'clock a.m. in the cathedral church of the Immaculate Conception at Ouidah for the repose of his soul, as also at the feasts, wakes and funeral games during the months of January, February, March.

As though the funeral games were that moment in progress, six bucks, tall black shining, in white flannels and open shirts, in a clap of sudden thunder leapt sideways on the stage, stamping with frantic limbs with six girls after them about half their height, whose knees knocked and jigged, whose bodies shuddered and twitched, whose eyes flashed and hands waves. Suddenly like a heavy river mist, a white cloud burst loudly, filling the room with aromatic smoke, obscuring everything. It cleared, the stage was empty again and his head was rocking. His body held colloquy with itself. You are laid in the deep low vault...sleep is falling heavy as a hand. His every fibre yearned after the creaking receding feet, yet he was deeply reassured. A light focused his attention. A monotonous far drip of water was marvellously reassuring. He had surrendered again. She was by his side.

He played idly with his full glass, then placed an empty glass upon it and when that seemed solid, another. His friends were looking at him in pleased fear. He added another. That too held. He saw they were afraid, they moved half back along their seats, stealthily and not to shake the table, and their eyes were riveted on the bulging transparent column in which lights glinted and lees of wine were solid as topaz. Only the snake-woman sat still and tired, her head drooping, her snake still too. The column reached now to his shoulder and he stood up, taking more glasses and building higher till again it was at his shoulder. His friends had shrunk still further from him, but a surging mass of black and white faces hung like a necklace before him, ebbing to and from him, growing smaller, larger; the eyes, teeth, winking enamels. Then he was oblivious of them, and then suddenly they cut his consciousness. His hand, his eye, his being were miraculously sure, adding glass to glass upon the slightly trembling column. That power, he felt, gave him power over Angela. He felt her eyes were focused on him, herself yearning to him as he had so often felt them before. She walked on sand where the sea ebbed, watching a ship bear him away, the afternoon falling grey about her, turning disconsolately to the cobbles of Boulogne, Calais.

Her eyes were glued on him yet darting sideways, compelled to watch him in unwilling admiration, but her body shrank back along the seat in fear the column fell and splintered round her. Then it was too high and he got up on the bench. Its every vibration was part of him, its every stress; each nerve, each muscle was in tune with it. Suddenly he was addressing her, them, himself. Gentlemen, here is our life. Her life begins here — this bottom glass. How full it is, how solid it begins (his voice clucked in wonder). It climbs, begins to sway. This top glass is quite empty, there is no deception. How it trembles, makes all tremble, and if it falls must bring all down, destroy what it started with. This glass that empty sways was me. Slowly I filled from her, grew solid and swayed less. Still the column sways, yet is a column — indivisible. But who built it, she or I or both, and then, what then?

A dozen hands held glasses out to him. How add to my own life which must move down. But how not add to her? Glass must grow to glass, she moves from water into air, yet then to water again. This column is alive with her. And if I take some down, shall we be where we started? I went so far to

171

meet her, in such currents fought. But she says yes, I must add glass to glass? With a horrified gesture, Angela, whose eyes had been glued on him in unwilling sombre admiration, cried no, leaping to stay his hand. For a moment the column swayed, grew stable, and, shuddering, fell upon itself, splinters flying into the room. The wine in the bottom glass bulged, slowly crept down its sides.

A blast of cold air was blowing through the room, the spectators moved to their seats. With anguish they looked at each other. They had come out of a dark warm place.

Her love, her protection, her sudden penitence and cry of why did you flowed over him. Something had got through, for a moment both had understood. Yet she would forget again. She would forget again. Why did what he gave her seem so precious once he had given it. No, that was not true, he forgot it then, but could not forget that she must treasure it. Yet it was no use to him without her, that was deeply true. How could he blame her for evading the responsibility of his love for her, since even he could not bear its weight, since for him it had no weight. Why did he seek the same law for male and female. Even were he both, it would be better for him to assume a masculinity, contained and non-existent, to compel her. But that was not true either, for he fought, struggled against, then submitted to, the imposition of her love upon him, that love she could not hold within herself and which was of no use to her.

Yet she would not submit. She bowed his head, but not her own, and absorbed, picked mushrooms in the wood. That was why. not time made her forget, not crumbling rocks and bursting vegetation piling upon what he thought the bleak crest of his love; but like a zephyr she forgot and like a zephyr warmed him or puffed sheltering clouds about him. What passion made him try to make permanent what he felt? Grave it not in stone nor brass but on eternity; another, his eternity. Feelings which anything might make thin or spout forth in thick blood. Yet the spirit swelled, took flesh; the mind lived, each skeleton was set out solid for an eternity. That chain was swung from star to star.

Yet he forgot too. The brains secretion a slime, oozing over, preserving, but deep hiding. In polar wastes among furious icy winds, a man kicks a ball, is alive, and for a moment some lens etches him, and makes him live again as often as a screen projects him to his fellows squatting in London or New York. He lives again among the young, the lovely, their tears of pity the blood his thirsting shade drinks to live again. That is now his life?

What then? The next day, from its cave some furious wind whistled up snow and ice and arctic night invaded him. So much for him. He was a thing whose edges waving caught the light, flashed for a moment; the movement dies, the light fades, he is himself again, transparent, water.

She played about his peaks and far below an obscure tumult of her penetrated. His roots were in deep caves, where boulders curving like huge thighs, still left a rift for him to creep through. Some murmur of trickling water, slimy moss, made walking difficult; the stairs were steeply treacherous.

In the enormous cavern the craggy roof stretched far where rare light gilded the withdrawn stalagmites, hieratic and most solemn.

A limpid river, cold to touch, flowed secretly a long way; the flat boats, crammed with faces blank in a remote unseeing dream cross each other; their helmsmen bearded, braced against their all too heavy lusts; while over them their demons soar batlike under the roof. His roots went down with joy, but she could not follow, could not leave earth, where, culling berries, herbs, the smell of hay, the croaking of frogs, which, like tiny bells, or distant, like a belated train, or like the cawing of crows, mingled in an immense languorous rattle under the moon; nor leave the deafening cry of grasshoppers shuddering in the burning noon, nor lambs nuzzling with frantic tails, cows leaping, butterflies coupling; the deep mist of living. She lived. It was so simple. Death, joy, dishonour, sickness, how foresee, evade or work for. Live! The sum the same. Drink and drugs quickened her stigmata diaboli. Yet she had tried to come down with him: it was stronger than herself. Sometimes she had felt herself going, a deep singing in her ears, her head grown monstrous light, her senses singing upwards, her body swaying, about to take flight into the earth. On an immense wave she relinquished herself. But that settled with a shock and she was on earth.

And he yearning sunward was justified in her, and her impossibility to be ought else. She had so tried but could not. Yet had she reached down to him, then she must go blank to him, grown part of him. But in her loves, her wilful blowing, he lived vicariously, and, though he resented it, he could not forego that necessity. His immobility found its life in her. He had lent her out then. He was her cully and profited by her. He would take her again, with all her profit his. So that, not conscious, yet inward knowing, he had turned her from him, unlaced each twining tendril, loosened each thorn, turning himself from her, darkening his face, her tendrils shivering on the blank air, uncertain where to turn.

Another sun then rose for her.

And for no, or every, reason, his heart began to beat violently, he was suddenly furious with her; her sombre face beside him, no longer a sick childs, moving out and away from him, fixed in night, filled him with rage. Whatever happened, she would always be herself, and nothing he could do could break that charmed circle, floating before around away.

His head was swimming, the floor heaving, his jaws clenched tight, the shapes in the room swaying round him. Staggering, he went from the room, half fell down stairs, was bundled into his coat, then into a taxi.

A blast of cold air woke him in confusion. He saw a canal and white in moonlight, swaying trees; half came to himself, stammering. The shimmer of water was asphalt, the trees lamp posts, he saw his hotel door. His hands undressed him, disposed of his clothes, cleaned his teeth, brushed his hair, while he staggered in the room. He fell into bed.

He had lost her again.

His head was two large hemispheres gliding in oil deliberately against each other with an unendurable irresistible motion, his whole being whining and shivering away from them, yet they expanded, filling the room, and somewhere in their side, hidden in deep undergrowth, were his mouth and working lips, a tiny hole. Time was passing with a frightful conscious rapidity. His imagination buzzed with images, sounds, too large for it; his eyes opening in delirium and seeing nothing, were comforted by a sword of fire, a beam of light which shot into the wardrobe mirror, his head and all in it, moving with a frightful and hurried apprehension. Suddenly wideawake, he stood in the room. What cry had called him?

She crouched dark on the floor, and when he put his arms round her she was trembling. That was unendurable; his heart melted, pouring over her. She fought him, feebly clinging, but he put her on the bed, undressed her awkwardly, his impotence puzzling him. She threw her arms round him, now Im happy. So he had held her trembling where sudden mistral howled icy among age-old ruins. They, too, had held the fairest and the best. She was talking to him and his heart dragged after her words. Forgive me. I did want to smash it. I was afraid it could stand another glass, that would have ended everything... do, do forgive me. And I didnt want to leave you....I dont know how I could. But I was frantic. It didnt seem to matter who I was with. It was so cold and bright. I was so restless. There was something I must find. Somewhere in some shop, among bric-a-brac, through some street. I was so confused, so unhappy, in despair. I must have bought so much — for a moment it all seemed what I wanted — Ill show you them. You can have them if you like. No you cant. I threw them away. It was better so, they took me from you. Her voice was tender, infinitely caressing, not what he imagined he remembered it. Shuddering to think how nearly he had lost her — with her voice all went — he clung to her, yet could not press her close. I was beastly to him, couldnt go to bed. I went on looking all the time, dragged him round the town, one shop and then another, he was so nice and then so tired. We sat in cafés, people came in, went out, once there was a fight, it got late, the patron looked cross. I simply couldnt go. I tried so hard to be nice to him, but there was always something I had to face — find, I mean. You were always looking at me. Now Ive come back.

He was falling asleep. There was a cave. She stood in darkness among others. Their rotting skin was leather, their mouldy lungs were leather. Some vapour had tanned her, but not him. She wore an apron of brown paper.

And for a long time he saw her vacillating in light in dark   receding always

Dec 1925 — May 1926

174

Appendices

APPENDIX A

The Theatre

The theatre is the staging for emotion; has been, must be....
  Emotion invariably translates itself into action, immediate or deferred;
Never in words.
  Words are a waste product of emotion and do not concern it.
  Thus the intellectual drama is not drama at all.
  It is the 'acting version' of a novel.
  This much for Shakespeare.
  The new school Strindberg. — Tchekhov.

*   *   *

  A fool is not known as such by his words.
  His actions are the clue to his madness.
  Similarly the hero, the villain.
  The secret springs which move them and which the dramatist considers
himself bound to expose have but a literary value and do not concern us when
shown on the stage.
  The idea that they interest even is mistaken.
  A successful play however is a valuable property.
  There are also actors and actresses.
  A play of pure emotion would need a tithe of the present cast of a play,
a hundredth of the expense in staging....
  Hence its impracticability.

*   *   *

  The successful playwright, Shakespeare, Tchekhov later, discovered
that without action of some sort, no play 'will go'. That is, a play without
some spectacular interest. No two senses may be concentrated without one
losing somewhat in intensity. A sonata cannot be criticised and heard
intensely at the same moment. Nor the music of a ballet when the choreo-
graphy is overloaded.
  The only form of drama which evades these mistakes is that made by
'Marionettes'. That is, conventionalised figures which do not draw attention
to their idiosyncrasies; placed in a neutral environment which does not
detract from the evocation of pure emotion.

177

For hundreds of years this has been understood.
It must not be lost sight of.

THE EVOCATION OF RACE MEMORIES

Art no longer attempts to elevate. So rare indeed is it to meet one who believes in a utilitarian art that it was a profound shock for me to hear lately, 'but I don't see what use your poetry is.'

Not attempting to elevate, Art becomes entirely a factor for the suggestion of emotions; thoughts.

With the old artists, too often it was merely a hitting of the same nail after it had impinged, thus driving it into a groove where the vibrations were deadened instead of merely a first tap which would have caused the whole of the receptive material to vibrate (the liberation of a complex).

It is conceivable that a smell of musk wafted through a theatre would affect an audience more poignantly, more profoundly, than anything they had before then experienced. For all plays are amenable to intellectual criticism of whatever kind. Hamlet need not affect a single member of the audience who does not wish it. This insidious smell of musk penetrates deeper into the mind through the senses, until the body is rapt into those vague splendid imaginings which are the flutterings of memories of man and the earth when they were young.

Who knows why a leaf pittering along a starlit path fills one with a sense of impending tragedy which surpasses all the poignancy made by poets telling of loves? An empty stage, quite dark; the rustling of a few leaves — I can conceive nothing which could affect me more poignantly, more profoundly.

I want to take a theatre in London, using for the plays either human marionettes of the Dutch-doll type or naked humans, or to clothe them in a sort of cylindrical garment. The plays will be the completion of a cycle dealing with the primitive emotions, of which Fear is one, these being I think the simplest for the evocation of race memories. The Margaret Morris theatre in Chelsea might be procured fairly cheaply, and it is cosy and intimate. About £20 would pay for two shows and I should be glad to hear from readers who are interested and how much they are prepared to contribute to such an end.

The Egoist 1,21 (2 November 1914)

APPENDIX B

Collected Poems 1912-1925*

Collected Poems 1912-1925 reprinted twelve poems from *Hymns* and six from *Poems* together with ten uncollected poems, two of which had not previously been published. Rodker's selection was fastidious, the self-criticism of a poet who had ceased to write poems, yet the standards referred to in his prefatory Note allowed him also to put on record, as a body of work marked by integrity of purpose, and as an epoch of the writer's life, a history of his career as a poet from start to finish. In keeping with such a design the poems are dated on the Contents page, and these dates are given in the notes which follow, although they do not always accord with other evidence. Some punctuation was lightly but inconsistently changed, but minor alterations of this sort (which may have been the work of the Curwen Press compositors) have not been recorded except where they are part of substantive textual revisions.

A NOTE
For this book I have chosen such of my poems as best seem to me to have come off. Those omitted were too forced, or did not satisfy my present standards. One thing this collection makes me realize very clearly is how much influenced I was by the French Poetry of 1850-1910. That was because I first came to poetry through that language (the foreign-ness already evocative and moving; which with its content satisfied my particular demand for what poetry ought to be). But until this had happened I was closed to English poetry, so that perhaps later it was too late to write poetry that would be nearer the traditions of the language I was using. *Pieta*, however, seems to me to have some of the good things of both languages. One gratifying thing about these poems is that they do get better with the years, but I have to ask myself why after 1925 I wrote no verse. Firstly I should say, because what remained of this impulse found relief in the writing of prose; and again, because the particular concentration, the state of feeling which conceived this kind of poem, came more rarely with maturity, possibly because at all times it was a difficult world to live in, and I was no longer prepared to live in it. Certainly this impulse now turns more readily into other channels in which to find, I will not say a completer gratification, but anyhow a more available form of it. It seems to me now, not to go more deeply into the matter, that when I wrote poetry I was, as it were, hanging in the void, and

* Paris: The Hours Press, 1930

these poems are my efforts to establish contact, indeed this need is the one thing the poems express, in 1912 as in 1925; and it is as true of the jokes as of some whose main function, I remember, when they were written, was to shock. They shocked me as much as they did some readers and reviewers, but I had the compensation of being the initiator of that assault. That these still shock me is a sufficient comment on their author at this moment, and because of it, my choice has had to be responsible. Yet some of these poems, which partly I should have liked to omit, do seem to me successful in their 'genre', and so they are included, excessive as, at this date, they seem. I think this much apology is needed — but only this much. The now-self for the then-self to the speculative reader.

1930

Contents. 1912: 'A Slice of Life'; 1913: 'The Gas Flame'; 1914: 'Sleep-Sick', 'To the London Sparrow', 'Vibro-Massage', 'The Descent into Hell', 'The Searchlight'; 1915: 'The Dancer Dancing', 'Inventory of Abortive Poems', 'Under the Trees' [*Hymns*], 'Hymn to Friends and Enemies' ['Hymn to Himself (Atlas 20th Century)']; 1916: 'Hymn of Hymns', 'Three Poems', 'Frogs'; 1917: 'Two Prison Poems' ['From a Biography' I & II]; 1919: 'Theatre', 'Deserted Wife', 'Dancer', 'Wax Dummy in Shop Window', 'The Pale Hysterical Ecstasy', 'Wild West Remittance Man', 'Southern Syncopated Singers', 'Pieta'; 1920: 'War Museum — Royal College of Surgeons'; 1921: 'Married'; 1925: 'To a Renault in the Country', 'Lines to an Etruscan Tomb', 'Out of the Water'.

'The Gas Flame'
13 little weary spire] weary spire. . . .
14 *omitted*
Stanza breaks between lines [14]-15, 18-19, 25-26, 28-29.

'The Searchlight'
3   wandering] moving
5   while] when   living,] living:
6   better to] to better
7   had —] had
8   kisses —] kisses . . .
9   great] blind
13 lost to her,] lost,
14 grief.] pain
14-15 *no stanza break*
17-18 *stanza break*
20 vain] vain,

'Hymn to Friends and Enemies'
This version of 'Hymn to Himself' follows the manuscript version dated October 1916, originally titled 'ATLAS . . . 20th Century'.

Hymn to Friends and Enemies:
        Atlas, twentieth century

Bilge
of sneers, insults:
kindnesses and obligations;
evil:
by me and to me —
squelches inside me.

No purge expels it,
it swinks in the hulk
like a ball of
plaster-of-paris
in a rat.

I can't keep going long
with that inside me.

8   swinks in] follows each movement of   (MS)
12   going] floating   (MS)

        'Frogs'
4   quick within] Quick in

        'Pieta'
1   the gay body] the body
17   knee.] knees.
17-18 *stanza break*
19   has pressed] presses
20   dust —] dust

        'Lines to an Etruscan Tomb'
1   heart] heart,
2   light. Light] light, light
7   dark I] dark, I
9   flying,] flying;
10   caught her, he was grimmer, beneath] Somewhat grimmer, caught up.
         Beneath.
12   shoved in] he shoved

        'Out of the water'
2   dies;] dies
4   dies:] dies
12   *omitted*
13   For glassy it holds in] Glassy it held
14   which festers   eats] which festered   ate
16   speaks] spoke

181

NOTES

INTRODUCTION

1.   *Poems*, to be had of the Author: 1 Osborn Street, Whitechapel [1914]; *Hymns*, London: The Ovid Press, 1920; *Montagnes Russes*, Paris: Librairie Stock, 1923; *The Lay of Maldoror* [translation], London: The Casanova Society, 1924; *Dartmoor*, Paris: Editions du Sagittaire, 1926; *The Future of Futurism*, London: Kegan Paul, Trench, Trubner & Company, [1927]; *Adolphe 1920*, London: The Aquila Press, 1929; *Collected Poems 1912-1925*, Paris: The Hours Press, 1930; *Memoirs of Other Fronts* [published anonymously], London: Putnam, 1932.

2.   Ezra Pound, 'Foreword to the Choric School', *Others* 1,4 (October 1915).

3.   Ezra Pound, letter to Margaret Anderson, 11 June 1917, in *Pound / The Little Review: The Letters of Ezra Pound to Margaret Anderson*, edited by Thomas L. Scott, et al., London: Faber and Faber, 1989.

4.   Ezra Pound, letter to Wyndham Lewis, and Wyndham Lewis, letter to Ezra Pound, both before July 1915, in *Pound / Lewis: The Letters of Ezra Pound and Wyndham Lewis*, edited by Timothy Materer, New York: New Directions, 1985. The poems compared were 'Portrait of a Lady' and 'The Dutch Dolls'.

5.   Ezra Pound, letter to Harriet Monroe, 30 September 1914, in *The Letters of Ezra Pound*, edited by D.D. Paige, London: Faber and Faber, 1951.

6.   Photocopies of Joseph Leftwich's diary are deposited in the Imperial War Museum and Tower Hamlets Libraries. The original is among his papers in the Central Zionist Archives, Jerusalem.

7.   *The New Age* XI,1 (7 November 1912).

8.   *Poetry and Drama* 1,1 (March 1913).

9.   *The Egoist* 1,21 (2 November 1914).

10.   There is nothing to suggest that Rodker's Dutch Dolls derive from Florence Upton's books for children. To all intents they are the generic wooden dolls with articulated legs. However, it is likely that Rodker, who discussed Bomberg's paintings in 'The "New" Movement in Art' (*The Dial Monthly* II,17 [May 1914]), was up to date with his friend's press cuttings. Richard Cork (*David Bomberg*, New Haven and London: Yale University

Press, 1987) cites a contemporary reviewer's comment on Bomberg's *Vision of Ezekiel* which may have prompted Rodker's use of the term: 'Dutch dolls engage in an elaborate gymnastic act in imitation of a Greek fret.' (*The Athenaeum* [21 February 1914].) This may be no more than a journalist's off-the-cuff remark, but it serves nevertheless to raise the question of emotional affinity in the work of Rodker and Bomberg.

11 Rutland Boughton, John Rodker, *Immanence*, London: Curwen Edition, 1920.

12. 'The Choric School', *Others*, loc. cit.

13. 'The Choric School', *The Drama* [Chicago], (August 1916).

14. Philip Heseltine, letter to Frederick Delius, 11 October 1916, in Cecil Gray, *Peter Warlock: A Memoir of Philip Heseltine*, London: Jonathan Cape, 1934.

15. Ezra Pound, letter to Wyndham Lewis, before July 1915, in *Pound / Lewis*.

16. S. Winsten, *Chains*, London: C.W. Daniel, 1920.

17. Julian Bell (ed.), *We Did Not Fight: 1914-1918 Experiences of War Resisters*, London: Cobden Sanderson, 1935.

18. *The Switchback*, i.e. *Montagnes Russes* (cf. note 1.)

19. Letter to Ezra Pound, 24 October 1930. Ezra Pound Papers, Yale.

20. Harold Loeb, letter to John Rodker, 11 July 1922. *Broom* Correspondence of Harold Loeb, Princeton.

21. Cited in Ellen Williams, *Harriet Monroe and the Poetry Renaissance*, Urbana: University of Illinois Press, 1977.

22. ' "Exiles", A Discussion of James Joyce's Plays', *The Little Review* V,9 (January 1919). It is likely that Rodker acquired his early knowledge of psycho-analysis from Barbara Low, whom he knew as early as 1914; her *Psycho-Analysis, A Brief Account of the Freudian Theory* was published in 1920.

23. Pound regarded William Carlos Williams's *The Great American Novel* (1923) and *Adolphe 1920* as the only two 'offspring' from *Ulysses* of any value. 'The Adolphe, professedly taking its schema from Benjamin Constant, brings the Joycean methodic inventions into a form; slighter than Ulysses, as a rondeau is slighter than a canzone, but indubitably a "development," a definite step in general progress of writing, having as have at least two other novels by Rodker, its definite shaped construction.' ('Dr Williams' Position', *The Dial* LXXXV,5 [November 1928].) Rodker's two other published novels at this time were *Montagnes Russes* and *Dartmoor*.

24. Clere Parsons, review of *Adolphe 1920, The Criterion* X,39 (January 1931).

25. Cited in William Lipke, *David Bomberg*, London: Evelyn, Adams and Mackay, 1967.

POEMS (1914)

Dedication: To SONIA

Copy text: *Poems* by John Rodker, To be had of the Author, 1 Osborn Street, Whitechapel [London, 1914].

Publication: 'The Poet to his Poems', 'The Music Hall', '...*for the Soul*', 'Under the Trees' II and III, 'Consummation', 'Sleep-Sick', *The Egoist* 1,10 (15 May 1914). 'The Mercury Vapour Lamps', *The Manchester Playgoer*, II,1 (July 1914). 'Spelled', 'The Storm', 'To the London Sparrow', 'Vibro-Massage', *The Egoist* 1,17 (1 September 1914). 'London Night', *Poetry* 5,3 (December 1914).

 'In the Strand'
In *Poetry* 'In the Strand' appears as the first section of 'London Night'.

 'London Night'
In *Poetry* the line 'To call her to my couch...' is bowdlerised to read 'To bring her to me.' In *Poems* the final lines of the *Poetry* version ('Night, speak me soft — / I have sipped but the rim of "her cup"... / Horror of vastness dripped / From star to star — / And even you / Could not help me. / I am afraid.') are abbreviated, perhaps in order to fit within the page.

 'The Descent into Hell'
Headnote: This poem should be read many times in order that the time-sense may become so essential a part of the poem as not to interfere with the sequence of the lines.

THEATRE MUET

Copy texts: 1-4, Ezra Pound (ed.), *Catholic Anthology*, London: Elkin Mathews, 1915; 5 and 7-10, *The Little Review* 4,4 (August 1917); 12, *The Little Review* 5,6 (October 1918); 6 and 11, *The Little Review* 6,3 (July 1919).

Dated MSS: 8, 13 February, 1917; 9, 14 February, 1917.

Publication: In his manifesto 'The Theatre' (see Appendix A), published in *The Egoist* 1,21 (2 November 1914), Rodker's proposal for a theatre of pure emotion includes 'Fear' as a specimen scenario for the dumb show of human puppets he envisaged. Pound included 'Fear' in his *Catholic Anthology* together with 'The Lunatic' and 'Twilight' I and II. 'Twilight' I and 'The Lunatic', together with the first series of 'The Dutch Dolls', also appeared in the issue of *Others* (October 1915) devoted to The Choric School. The title 'Theatre Muet' (without accents) was first used for the series of five pieces published in *The Little Review* 4,4 (August 1917): 'Interior', II 'Hunger', III (here 8), IV 'To S.E.R.', V (here 10). Another piece (here 12) appeared with the title 'Theatre Muet' in the group of 'Prose Poems' by Rodker published in *The Little Review* 5,6 (October 1918). Two other pieces, numbered 6, 'The End of the World', and II, 'The Bowed Head' were published under the heading 'Theatre Muet' in *The Little Review* 6,3 (July 1919).

Manuscript evidence connects the four pieces published in *Catholic Anthology* and the eight published in *The Little Review*. Three incomplete manuscript versions exist: A. a series of typed and autographed mss numbered 2-4, 8, 9, X, and [XII cancelled] XI; B. three typed mss numbered 7-9; C. typed mss of 'Interior' and 'The End of the World' with the autograph title 'Two Plays'. Where they overlap A. and B. and the series of five pieces in *The Little Review* follow the same sequence but with different series of numbers. The relationship can be more clearly presented in tabular form:

A.	B.	LR
8	7	III
9	8	IV
X	9	V

The arrangement of 'Theatre Muet' adopted here is based on A. The ordinal numbering [I]-V in *The Little Review* 4,4 (August 1917) is disregarded as editorial, but the numbers 6 and II in *The Little Review* 6,3 (July 1919) are accepted as authorial, except that what is ostensibly Roman II is taken to be a typographical misrepresentation of Arabic 11. Cancellation of XII in A. is also disregarded as a local adjustment of ordinal numbering. On this reasoning numbers 1 and 7 remain unaccounted for, but 'Hunger' can be identified as 7 on the basis of its position in the group of five pieces published in *The Little Review*, and it is logical to identify 'Fear' as the first piece in the series as a whole.

As a reconstruction this arrangement is speculative as well as conjectural, since 'Theatre Muet' is not self-evidently an integral work. The pieces fall into two groups on the basis of dates of composition and publication, and the title is associated in the first instance with the later group, although Rodker adopted it in A. as an autograph superscript title for 'The Lunatic' and 'Twilight' I and II. 'Theatre Muet' might more appropriately then be considered as the generic term for a particular type of writing. It is also possible that the term was contributed editorially by Ezra Pound in his role as foreign editor of *The Little Review*. As a type of writing for the theatre these experiments of Rodker's appear to have influenced at least one writer: Alfred Kreymborg, the editor of *Others*, published two collections of plays for human puppets, *Plays for Poem-Mimes* (New York, 1919) and *Puppet Plays* (London, [1923]), the latter with a preface by Gordon Craig.

THE DUTCH DOLLS

Copy texts: *Others* 1,4 (October 1915); Part II, MS *Syrups*.

Dated MSS: 'Finis!', 1914; 'Columbine Thinks of Marrying', 'Time's Healing', May 1915; 'Envoi to Columbine', 1917.

Publication: Part II, nos. 2 and 3, as 'Dutch Dolls, Second Series', *The Little Review* 6,3 (July 1919).

Rodker wrote to Harriet Monroe, the editor of *Poetry*, on 26 April 1915, to offer the first series of fifteen poems; Wyndham Lewis had offered to take numbers 9 and 12 for *Blast*, but he wanted the series published as a whole. After placing the series with *Others* he wrote to Monroe again, on 7 October 1915, to offer a second series of 'The Dutch Dolls' numbering eight poems. (Both letters in the *Poetry* archives, University of Chicago Library.) The second series referred to does not correspond to Part II in MS *Syrups* in at least two respects, since the latter consists of seven poems, and the final poem is dated 1917.

SKETCHES AND PROSE POEMS

Copy texts: 'Monkeys', 'Possession', MS; 'Three Nightpieces', *The Little Review* 4,3 (July 1917); 'Incidents in the Life of a Poet', *The Little Review* 4,9 (January 1918); 'Theseus', 'Dancer', 'God', *The Little Review* 5,6 (October 1918); 'God Bless the Bottle', *The Little Review* 6,4 (April 1919); 'Chanson on Petit Hypertrophique', *The Little Review* 7,2 (July-August 1920); 'Mr. Segando and the Fifth Cataclysm', *The Tyro* No. 1 (1920).

Ezra Pound suggested 'Sketches by John Rodker' as a heading for 'Three Nightpieces' and a 'Theatre Muet' piece (see Thomas L. Scott and Melvin J. Friedman [eds.], *Pound/The Little Review*, London: Faber, 1989, 74-5). The heading 'Prose Poems' for the three pieces published in *The Little Review* 5,6 (October 1918) is presumably editorial, perhaps citing a precedent: six prose poems by Arthur Rimbaud, translated by Helen Rootham, had appeared in the July 1918 issue.

'Monkeys'
Autograph revision of typed manuscript in four sections titled 'Zoo'. The first section (below) was deleted and the title changed.
Zoo
1.
She was tiny — very fragile — dressed by Reville. Her eyes suffusing love, she leant heavily on her lover's arm while from under the black comb of his bowler he beamed at her through pince-nez.

It was summer. Her white clothes fluttered gaily.

They stopped before the Mandril's cage and became suddenly distraught, tracing the ferocious violet and red markings upon its face. Enwrapt in the contemplation of bizarre and seemingly inexplicable colour she did not heed him when he plucked her sleeve to draw her away.

The Mandril wreathed back its lips scowling, then clumsily pivoting on its knuckles, turned its back to them.

There were the same colours on its rump, but in patches of sky blue, pink and yellow. Again they became tongue-tied. He began to feel uncomfortable, and tried to urge her away.

She suddenly nestled in to him, turning up the adorably fragile face, with its delicious snub nose, its pouting lips — and said timidly and blushing. —

'I'm so glad you're not like that.'

'Mr. Segando and the Fifth Cataclysm'
When Wyndham Lewis solicited Rodker's contribution to *The Tyro* he asked 'Have you ever dreamt of a perfect civilization, that would really suit you: so adjusting matter & society as to eliminate every emetic sight and makeshift person?' Rodker's satire on perfectibility has H.G. Wells for its object, rather than the ideas put forward by Lewis in *The Caliph's Design*, but by the time it appeared in *The Tyro*, almost two years later, Rodker's 'satire on Effort', as Lewis saw it, was more in tune with Lewis's views. (For Lewis's letters to Rodker see W.K. Rose [ed.], *The Letters of Wyndham Lewis*, Norfolk, Conn.: New Directions, 1963, 105-6, 124, 126.) 'Segando' is Lewis's substitution for 'Wells'.

HYMNS

Dedication: To M.B.

Copy text: *Hymns* by John Rodker, London: The Ovid Press, 1920.

Dated MSS: 'Pregnant', December 1915; 'Hymn to Cold', October 1916; 'Hymn to Death 1914 and On', December 1916; 'Hymn of Hymns', 1916; 'Gas Fire', February 1917; 'Wax Dummy in Shop Window', September 1918; 'Wild West Remittance Man', March 1919.

Publication: 'Hymn to Death 1914 and On', *The Egoist* 5,10 (November-December 1918); 'Under the Trees', *Poetry* 7,4 (January 1916); 'Chryselephantine', 'Wax Dummy in Shop Window', 'The Pale Hysterical Ecstasy', 'Wild West Remittance Man', *The Little Review* 6,3 (July 1919); 'Wild West Remittance Man', *The Apple* 1,1 (January 1920).

'Under the Trees'
Numbered IV in manuscript.

OTHER POEMS 1913-1927

Copy texts: MS; 'Hymn to Virginity III', *The Egoist* 5,5 (May 1918); 'Theatre', *Broom* 2,1 (April 1922); 'Pieta', *The Tyro* No. 2 (1922); 'War Museum — Royal College of Surgeons', *Collected Poems 1912-1925*, Paris: The Hours Press, 1930.

Dated MSS: 'Deidre is Dead', 1913-14; 'The Fair', 'The Acrobats', 1914; 'Snow Pieces', 6 February 1917; 'To Any Idol', 1915; 'Nude with Wrist-Watch', October 1916; 'Beatitude', 1916; 'Under the Trees VI', September 1916; 'The Searchlight', 1914; 'An Old Story', October 1916; 'Words', 1916; 'Hymn to Nature', October 1916; 'Hymn to Virginity', November 1916; 'Frogs', 1917-20; 'A CO's Biography', January 1918; 'Theatre', 1920; 'Married', 1920-21; 'Out of the Water', 1923; 'To a Renault in the Country', July 1926; 'Havre Cathedral', 18 October 1926; 'Often a Waitress', 1927.

Publication: 'Dead Queens', 'Because Some Lover'; 'In a Garden', *Poetry* 10,3 (June 1917); 'Spring Suicide', *The Future* (March 1917); 'In a Garden', 'Spring Suicide', *Others, An Anthology of the New Verse*, New York, 1917; 'The Searchlight', *Poetry* 15,1 (October 1919); 'Theatre', *Fanfare* 1,5 (1921); 'Southern Syncopated Singers', *The Tyro* No. 2 (1922), *The Little Review* 8 (Spring 1922); 'Married', *Contact* No. 5 (June 1923); 'To a Renault in the Country', 'Lines to an Etruscan Tomb', *Poetry* 30,5 (August 1927).

The poems have been arranged chronologically except that from 'Dead Queens' to 'Words' they follow the order in which they appear in MS *Syrups*.

    'Dead Queens'
The epigraph is adapted from Ezra Pound, 'The Seafarer'.
    'Atavisms'
Rodker was paid £4 for this poem by *Poetry*, but it was not published.
    'Beatitude'
Titled 'Obsession' in another manuscript.

ADOLPHE 1920

Copy text: John Rodker, *Adolphe 1920*, [London]: The Aquila Press, 1920.

Publication: *The Exile* No. 1 (Spring 1927); No. 2 (Autumn 1927); No. 3 (Spring 1928).